Fingerprints

BITS AND PIECES OF MOTHERHOOD

Compiled by
Lucille Martin

Fingerprints—
Bits and Pieces of Motherhood
compiled by Lucille Martin

Copyright © 2016

All rights reserved.

Library of Congress Number: 2016904340
International Standard Book Number: 978-1-60126-487-9

Printed 2016 by
Masthof Press
219 Mill Road
Morgantown, PA 19543-9516

Table of Contents

Acknowledgements vi

Summer Requirements 1
A Dream Family 6
A Virtuous Woman 8
Likeness 13
Bits & Pieces 14
No Flops, Please! 19
Changed Mind 20
Do I Really Love It? 21
Grow in Grace 25
Mommy and the Kangaroo Car 29
Grown Up 31
My Loaves 32
Out-of-Hand, Into His Hand 33
Learning by Doing 34
The Measure of My Days 35
Carol in July 36
These Are Our Children 37
While Folding Clothes 38
Weak, But Willing 39
God's Love 40
Kept Safely 41
First Glimpse 41
Life at Mountain Lane 42
The Potty Train 45
A Garden for the Children 46
My Race 48
Surrogate Mother 49

Surmounting Mom 51
Straight to My Father 53
Through a Glass, Darkly 54
Love Note 55
When He Can't Find the Pocket 56
Of Pacifiers and Prayer 58
On Moving 61
Bouncing Is Better 62
List, Revised 64
Let It Shine 65
Holding the Baby 66
Company Coming 67
Twin Song 69
One Mother 70
No Name for the Baby 71
The Mother Mender 75
Bewildered 76
Mother Love 78
Unborn Love 79
Little Blue Shoe—Lost! 80
Her Job in the Kingdom of God 82
All the Way to the "Son" 84
A Safe Shelter 86
On Bringing Up Difficult Children 87
Moving Along With Reality 88
Chatterbox 90
Barber Meditations 91
"Can I Laugh Ya?" 92
Is Your HOUSE Clean? 94
On Call 96
Humbling Realization 98
This Is Not That Bad 99
Why Didn't You Tell Me? 102
My House and God's 105
Beauty at Night 109
When the Thought Counts 111

Welcome	113
God Brought Us Home	114
A Reminder to Worship	116
From Faith to Sight	117
Sensation	118
My Loaves and Fishes	119
Why Do I Want to Be Well?	122
How to Do It All	126
Choicest Blessing	128
In the Garden	129
Is Being a Good Mom Good Enough?	131
Essence of Life	133
Lost!	134
Messy Morning	136
On Mother's Day	138
Applesauce and the Blame Game	142
Peace in the Midst of Sandy	144
Refocus	146
Squirrel for Snack, Anyone?	149
"Lest We Forget"	152
My Reality	156
The Mourning Dove Mother	158
The Things Mothers Do	160
Out of the Mouth of Babes	163
Dear Son	165
This Is Life	166
What Color Is Grass, Anyway?	170
What I Learned From the Birth of Our First Baby	173
Childish Trust	176
What If God Says No?	177
Solitude	179
Measured in Moments	182
Of Children and Floors	183
Dandelion Bouquets	184
Spend and Be Spent	185
Send Them to School With a Smile	186

A warm thank you to:

- The twenty-plus ladies who responded to my request for material, and filled my mailbox with envelopes from far and near. What a wonderful way to make new friends!

- Masthof Press, for being so easy to work with.

- My husband, who patiently helped me understand the computer as I typed and edited.

- All the friends who kept me inspired by expressing their interest in the book, and asking how the project was going.

- Meredith, Gina, Stephanie, Sue, and Aunt Grace for your helpful advice.

To God be the glory.

SUMMER REQUIREMENTS
by Sue Hooley

What doth the LORD require of thee?
To do justly, and to love mercy,
and to walk humbly with thy God.
-Micah 6:8

Compared to other places, northeast Washington is a difficult place in which to find fruit. So if someone discovers fruit at a good price, he will likely share that information. Such was the case last summer when peaches became available through a Hutterite colony. A sign-up sheet was posted at church on which we could write how many boxes of peaches we wanted to order.

I really wanted to can peaches. Since we moved the previous summer, I hadn't had the opportunity to restock my shelves with the normal amount of canned fruit and our supply had dwindled to a mere two dozen quarts.

But should I undertake this project? My two oldest children were working at a bakery. We were temporarily living in town, so the rest of the children were in the house all day long, plus my husband was working out of a home office. It was a daily challenge to keep the household operating smoothly.

Suddenly I had a mental battle. I wanted to go to that sign-up sheet and write "ten boxes for Hooleys." After all, we were one of the biggest families in church and somehow a big fruit order seemed like a part of my identity. A silent conversation began to go through my brain, "So, you are getting ten boxes of peaches…" I mentally argued the pros and cons. *Canned peaches would be convenient. Is it expedient to tackle this project in our present circumstances?* And all the while, flashing in imaginary black and white, was *ten boxes for Hooleys.*

I'm not always driven by accomplishments, and I'm not sure why this particular subject was so intense. Perhaps I wanted to be normal in our temporarily abnormal circumstances. After a talk with my practical husband, the facts became clearer. Sometimes we must make adjustments so we can cope better with our circumstances. There is more than one right way to provide food for a family

There is more than one right way to provide food for a family. Where had I heard that before? Suddenly a conversation from years ago came to my mind.

"Janet is sure that there will be ladies in heaven who never canned a peach," Molly related.

"Why did she say that?" I wondered.

"She was raised in the city and just in the last ten years have she and her husband become Christians. Now they are interested in finding a Biblical church. She is learning many godly principles and putting them to practice. She spends hours nurturing her children, reaching out to her unsaved family and learning to be a godly wife. She thinks gardening and preserving are awesome talents, but she can't imagine learning all of those cultural abilities, too."

"Cultural abilities?" I gasped.

"Think about it," Molly continued. "Much of our conversation centers on the things we do, house cleaning, preserving, etcetera. Perhaps we assume in all of our good busyness that our children will learn to be kind and obedient. Maybe we think we are being a good wife by doing these noble things, but maybe we haven't really learned to be a helpmeet to our husbands and a joyful mother of children. Janet helped me realize that the art of preserving food isn't the most important one to pass on to our children."

"But what do they eat in the winter?" I asked.

"They buy cases of whatever is on sale. Really, is that any different from buying ten boxes of peaches to can versus buying that many boxes of fresh fruit through the winter? There is more than one right way to provide food for our family."

"Sometimes we unintentionally equate good practices with godliness," Molly continued. "We can learn many homemaking skills that will benefit us throughout life, yet the Bible doesn't require specific homemaking skills to be a successful wife and mother. I guess we need to find a balance that fits our individual lives," Molly concluded.

In the busyness of summer, finding that proper balance can be difficult. No two summers are exactly alike, and what worked one year may suddenly become cumbersome during another one. Most of our children were born in April and June, and I soon decided that newborn babies and canning did not go well together. One summer I had young teens, younger children, and a new baby and to my surprise, I found that canning projects went fairly smoothly.

When I was a young mother, I heard a middle-aged woman offer this advice: "I want my teen-aged girls to be available to help young moms. It gives them added experience. But it bothers me when the mothers want voluntary help for specialty projects. I didn't preserve all kinds of relishes and jellies when my children were young; I did only what was necessary. Multiple preschoolers take a lot of time and energy and sometimes young mothers add to their frustration by heaping extra work on themselves and, then suddenly they are overwhelmed."

Her insight was heaven-sent. It became my guide as I planted a garden and preserved its harvest in the years following when our first children were young. It was mentally freeing to realize that it is reasonable to do only what is necessary for my stage of life and it is reasonable to ask for help if I really need it.

Sometimes a different approach helps simplify projects and makes work more enjoyable. A few years ago we decided to harvest the corn patch after supper. The younger children seemed to catch the "spirit of change" and they were not grumpy like I had anticipated. It worked so well that, by default, doing corn in the evening has become a family tradition. It's cooler, there are fewer bugs, and everyone is around to help and we have a good time. A few special snacks and drinks add a little extra spice to the evening. Processing corn from 5:00 p.m.-10:00 p.m. doesn't seem as formidable a task as starting the project in the morning.

Sometimes we need to make adjustments so we can deal with a crisis. My sister-in-law made a quick decision to cancel her peach order when her 5-year-old son broke his leg. The break required a body cast and he needed her undivided attention for a few days until life settled into a new routine. He will not remember whether or not there were peaches that year. But he will remember the time his mother took for him.

My friend Nellie bought several boxes of tomatoes to make into pizza sauce. About then, her baby developed a severe ear infection and she was on demand day and night.

"My husband helped me make pizza sauce on a rainy day when he did not need to go to work," she told me. "Throughout that pizza sauce process, the baby yelled frequently, and I stopped often to take care of her. Karl methodically ran the tomatoes through the strainer and it was a tremendous help.

"After a bit he asked, 'How much does a jar of pizza sauce cost?'

"'Ninety-nine cents, if I can find it on sale,' I told him. 'Why?'

"He went for the calculator and began to tally up the expenses. 'Do you realize you can buy it cheaper than you can make it?' he asked. 'This is expensive pizza sauce! Plus, the baby is cranky, the kitchen is messy and you are worn out. Why do you do it?'

"Why did I? Was it because my mom made pizza sauce? Did I think I was saving money? Did I like homemade better?" I finally blurted out, "'Every noble homemaker cans pizza sauce, plus I want to teach the art of canning to my children.'

"He gave me a funny grin and wittily presented some logical facts. 'I think the baby's ears hurt too badly for her to have learned anything today. Amanda is not a contented baby and she is even worse when she is sick. Perhaps you should wait to teach the art of canning to the children until they are old enough to help and understand. Maybe we need to compare sense to cents and make a decision accordingly.'

"So guess what?" Nellie asked with a twinkle in her eye. "I buy pizza sauce and I really don't mind. I was getting so frustrated trying to juggle everything. I was caught between caring for my children and doing what I thought every noble homemaker should do," she chuckled.

If we find ourselves overwhelmed with many summer responsibilities, perhaps we need to step back and try evaluating the situation from another perspective. Sometimes the simplest changes will give us a bit of space and we will be more relaxed and productive. If in doubt, your heavenly Father will give you wisdom to make choices that are best for you, this busy summer season (James 1:5).

Remember that sign-up sheet? I ordered just enough for fresh eating. They were flavorless and the meanest things to get off the pit.

A Dream Family
by Regena Weaver

Recently our oldest daughter shared a dream with us. That in itself is not unusual. In the past eight years I have frequently given an open ear to what went on in her subconscious brain. Often it was shared, between sobs, in the middle of the night, and was colored by her current fears of wolves, cobras and such like. Those were nightmares.

This was markedly different. In her dream our family was gathered around in the family room engaged in quiet activities such as reading, embroidery, and singing while rocking the baby. A cozy domestic scene. "We should do that sometime," she said wistfully.

Is it coincidence that this came at the close of an especially busy summertime? Family time revolved around garden activities and outdoor games. During the long daylight hours, leisure time catered to bike rides and hot dog roasts, not embroidering beside the fireplace!

However, now the garden has been put to bed for its winter hibernation. Darkness descends hours before even a tired first grader's bedtime. Bike rides and baseball practice hold no appeal in the sometimes sub-zero weather. Various times since that dream our family of six has spent a leisurely evening in the family room, sometimes with a roaring fire in the fireplace. "Yes," our daughter agrees, "this is almost like my dream." Teaching them the basics of playing crokinole (Is this a calm thing when there are 2 and 4 year olds helping?). Reading *Adventures of Danny Meadow Mouse* aloud to the three older ones.

Perhaps we are a "dream family" . . .

Actually, we are! God has blessed me with a loving Christian husband and four healthy children. We have a warm house. Our freezers and basement shelves are full of last summer's garden bounties. Our Christian friends would rally around us should we face reverses in life. Even our closest neighbors, though most of them are decidedly not Christians, are of that staunch neighborly "would-do-anything-to-help" sort that are read about in books from half a century ago.

To many of my contemporaries around the world, and no doubt many I meet when I go to the local grocery store, mine sounds like a dream existence. What does it matter that the paint is chipping on our dining room walls? Why wonder how we'll cope with the demands of our very welcome and anticipated 5th child into our already busy domestic schedules? Why worry about the one broken pane of glass in the family room window, when the plastic/storm window combination keeps the winter air out for now?

We are richly blessed. We have a dream family!

A Virtuous Woman
by S. Kreider

"SNAP!" I sighed. Another needle had met its doom. This was the third needle that I had broken in my last couple hours of sewing. *All in the name of virtuous,* I thought as I looked for another needle. I felt like giving it a warning of the doom it was sure to meet, but instead I removed the broken needle and stuck the new one in its place. Things went much better for awhile, at least I thought, until I removed the half-sewn garment from my sewing machine and looked at my handiwork. My hopes of a neatly sewed dress faded rapidly. There in front of me lay a half completed dress. The skirt that I had so neatly tried to sew was far from being neat in reality. Extra tucks appeared here and there, and it was beyond me how they had managed to get in there. Frustration threatened to overcome me. To make matters worse, my children sounded frustrated too. *This is enough; it's not worth having a bad day simply because I thought I had to sew!*

My mind went back to the conversation I had had a couple of weeks ago after church. "I finally feel caught up," Jessica was saying. "I got all my summer sewing done now plus sewed a bunch for next school year and so...whew, that sure was a good feeling. Oh, it just felt so virtuous!" She looked at the rest of the ladies.

"I know the feeling," another mom, Renae, replied. "I love getting my sewing caught up and our children always love it; it's so much fun to play with all the spools of thread . . ." her voice trailed off. Then looking at me, Renae asked, "So what have you been doing, Beth? I know you don't sew, so what are you busy with?"

I jerked my attention back to the conversation and found myself replying. "Oh," I laughed, "I know I don't sew, but it seems like I still keep busy. I do bookwork and runs for the business besides the regular stuff, so I'm not lacking work!" I laughed lightly. Somehow I thought it sounded rather lame.

"I see; I can't imagine what I would do if I wouldn't sew, but then again, your house is probably cleaner than mine." Renae chuckled, and soon our little group of ladies had dispersed. But during the next couple of days, my mind was in a turmoil. *Should I try to sew again?* I hadn't tried for about a year, and maybe this time things would be different. Maybe, for once, everything would turn out as beautifully as I envisioned. How nice it would be to be able to tell the ladies what clothes I had managed to sew in only a few short hours. Hmmm, wouldn't they be impressed that I had finally learned? Yes, I would prove that I too could be "virtuous."

That night I had told my husband Kyle my plans. He agreed that it wouldn't hurt to try again, but he was concerned that I thought that that was the only way to be virtuous. "You do a wonderful job of keeping our little family happy and clean and fed, so to me you are the most virtuous woman I could find!" He smiled as he gave me a little hug.

So began my sewing endeavors. I purchased some fabric, and very carefully and precisely cut out a dress for myself. I did need a few new dresses, and here was a piece that would work just fine as a trial. A couple of days later, I tackled the job. Here I was, a frustrated mom with frustrated children, plus an upside-down house! I went downstairs and after settling the argument, I said, "Come on children. Let's go read a story."

Cheers of joy erupted, and then Abigail said, "Mom, I thought you said you had to sew all day today."

I laughed. "Yes, I know I said that, but I think I'll stop for today because you all sound like you need a Mom to take care of you, so why don't we read for a bit, and then we can all clean up the house together!"

Hours later, the house was in tip-top shape with wafts of supper filling the air. Soon Devin and Abigail were both running toward the window. "I think I hear Dad!" Devin shouted. This was definitely our favorite part of the day. The children had learned to hear those first sounds of Kyle's truck coming down the road. After the children had told him their highlights of the day, Kyle looked at me and said, "So, how did your sewing project go?"

"Absolutely terrible," I replied and informed him of my disastrous day. "Guess I'll just have to be content to not be one of those 'virtuous' women who crank out beautifully-sewn garments one after another, because after what happened today, I'll be quite content to let Jane sew them."

"Well, that's just fine; you obviously gave it an honest try, and that's what counts. Plus Jane needs the income, so let her sew them, and by the sounds of things, we'll all be happier!"

I nodded and wholeheartedly agreed! Jane was a single sister in the church who sewed for her living. I knew she was a wonderful seamstress, and had asked her if she would like to sew for me, since needless to say, sewing was definitely not one of my talents. She had been eager for the job and how glad I was to have properly sewn clothes that actually fit, not with the neckline pulled funny, and the cape hung sadly to one side.

• • • • •

A feeling of excitement was in the air. I wasn't sure what was going on, but something obviously was. Soon Cherilyn plopped a little envelope into my hand. I took it and concluded that this must be the reason for the excitement. After we got home from church that night, I opened the envelope. *Hmmm, this did look interesting.* "Another Tupperware party?" Kyle asked teasingly.

"No, it's actually a farewell tea party for Marla. Remember she's leaving for the Dominican Republic in two weeks, so Cherilyn and Renae are planning a farewell for her. It's next week Friday night; think you'll be able to babysit?"

Kyle didn't answer right away. "I'll try," he said and then continued, "it's mulch season for us, so we'll be really busy soon, probably starting next week. Usually we run late and hard, but I'll see what I can do."

I nodded. I knew what he meant. I hadn't been married to Kyle all these years in vain. I knew when the pressures of the season were upon us, he worked hard and did his utmost to keep up with the demanding work. Still, deep down I had a feeling that everything would work out. After all, it wasn't every day that the ladies from church had an outdoor tea party!

• • • • •

The Friday for the tea party arrived, and clear skies and warm sunshine made the day unspeakably gorgeous! At four o'clock the phone rang. It was Kyle. He sounded awfully dejected. "What's happened?" I managed to squeak out.

"Honey, I'm so sorry. I'm in Caridon, and I have engine trouble, so I'm going to need you to run down to Harv's Repair, and pick up parts and bring them to me. I already talked to Harv about it, and they are going to send the right tools and parts with you."

Tears smarted my eyes. *Kyle wanted me to run to Caridon with parts? Why, that was a 4½-hour drive one way. And today of all days . . .* Kyle continued, "Honey, are you there?"

"Ahh, yes, I heard what you said. I guess I was just trying to digest the info; you know today was the farewell for Marla. But don't worry, I'll be fine." But my voice betrayed my discouragement, and Kyle knew I was struggling.

"I know. I'm so sorry; I really feel bad, but there's nothing else to do. I've thought about many different options before I called you. I'll call Bro. James to see if Daryl could come along with you to help me fix the truck." We planned some more, and after I hung up the phone, I desperately tried to be cheerful. I enjoyed running for parts and helping Kyle where I could, but this? I determined to make the best of it with God's help.

The ride was enjoyable, and Daryl enjoyed the excitement of getting out and seeing some country he had never seen before. Exactly 4½ hours after we had left home, we arrived at Caridon. We found Kyle's broken-down truck easily, and together we got to work. After getting the children fed and settled for some sleep, I joined Kyle and Daryl. By the sounds of things, they were enjoying themselves despite the circumstances. Daryl and I took turns holding the light for Kyle, and Kyle patiently pulled out one injector after the next until he found the faulty one. Then it was time to replace it with the new one. Finally at 2:30 a.m. we were done. Whew, what a job, and along the road at that.

The next morning the children and I drove home, and Kyle and Daryl finished their delivery before heading home as well. What an adventure it had been! Kyle thanked me profusely after he got home, and I told him I was glad I could help him out. Deep down I was truly thankful that God had helped me to focus on the exciting part of it, instead of on the fact that I missed the tea party.

• • • • •

Months flew by, and Christmas found us travelling the many miles to visit Kyle's folks who lived in North Carolina. It was always good to go and see all the friends and relatives, and catch up with everyone's lives again. The Weaver family gathering was no exception. It had been years since we had been able to attend, and we were glad to see all the ones that were there. We had just walked in when Kyle's cousin Tim remarked, "Hey Kyle, we really enjoyed the form letter that we got from you."

Kyle smiled and patted my shoulder and replied, "It's my

wife's doings. If it wasn't for her you'd never hear from us!" We all laughed and continued on our way.

Later I was enjoying a visit with Cindy, Tim's wife. "We really enjoyed your letter; I couldn't believe it, that you actually drove 4½ hours to go help Kyle fix his truck. I mean, what a true husband and wife team. How virtuous!!!"

I gulped. *What had she said? That I was virtuous for helping Kyle?* I could hardly believe my ears. Here I was trying hard to accept the fact that I was not a virtuous woman because I didn't know how to sew, but really, was sewing the only thing that made a woman virtuous? Why of course not! The realization hit me like never before. No, God had not given me the ability to sew, but God had called me to be a helpmeet for my husband, and He had also given me the ability to do many other things. Was I using these talents for His glory? Or was I so busy comparing myself with others and lamenting that I wasn't fit to serve Him, because I didn't have their talents? I knew that that wasn't what God wanted of me. He simply wanted me to use what I had for Him and for His glory!

LIKENESS

My daughter had gone on a weekend trip,
And coming home with smiling lip,
She told us the details as daughters do.
"And Mother, Suzanne's mom is much like you . . .
I thought of her sweetness and how she looked,
Or was it her words or the way she cooked?"
The end of the story surprised me too—
"She licked the spatula just like you!"

-MJZ

BITS & PIECES
by Stephanie (Funk) Leinbach

— PART 1 —

"Cassidy!" I called. "I want you to hang out these dishtowels."

My husband had put up a line just the right height for my little girls to help hang out the laundry. Anything that would not drag on their low line was their job to hang outside. Since I collect my dirty dishtowels until I have a small load, it was the perfect job for an eight year old.

About 15 minutes later, Cassidy entered the kitchen and shared what she had been pondering as she hung out the towels. "As I was hanging out the towels, I noticed I was getting close to the end of the line. Then I thought about how the end of the line was like getting to the end of life. I pictured each dishtowel as if it was one year in my life, and I counted them. There were 29 dishtowels, so that means I have 29 years in my life."

As her mother, I was never before so thankful for the extravagant amount of dishtowels that I own. It was a good reminder of how short life is. In my eight-year-old's mind, 29 years was a long time to live. However, as a 38 year old, I knew all too well how soon my oldest daughter was going to reach her 29th birthday.

— PART 2 —

There is nothing like a chuckle to rejuvenate your spirit.

One busy day, the baby Renae was fussing, and chaos reigned in the house. I grabbed the baby cereal box for a quick fix to quiet her. In spite of my hurried motions, I could not help but notice my seven year old's neat printing under the words, "Best if used by." She had written "Renae" just above the obscure date.

— PART 3 —

The Spirit of Obedience?

As a home-school mother, I corrected books whenever I had a spare moment. Often the children were deep in their play by the time I got around to checking their work. "Cassidy!" I called to my first grader playing with her sisters in the basement. "You got a few wrong that I want you to redo." She came willingly enough, but she made sure she brought her play telephone along. It would not be good to lose possession of that to the others.

As she sat at her desk correcting her work, I wasn't sure where her mind was. "Ding-a-ling, Ding-a-ling," she rang out.

"Cassidy!" I scolded. "You cannot do school and talk on the phone at the same time!"

"I know," she agreed. "That is why I am not answering it."

— PART 4 —

Haste Makes Trouble

As a mother of six, I often find myself trying to plan my agenda around time and children. Too often I feel the rush of life which controls my spontaneous actions or my hasty decisions. Too often I forget to allow time for the little extras that come with children—a hungry baby, a potty break, or an unexpected catastrophe.

This particular Saturday was planned. My husband and I would do our shopping trip together. When we went together, he would drop off three of the children with me at the store where I needed things, and he would go his way with the other three. To make it easy for him, I usually took the two youngest with the oldest to help, and he would take the three middle children.

However, as we were scurrying around getting ready to go, my almost six year old complained of a bellyache. A bellyache was not on the agenda, and I really wanted this trip to town. A few minutes later, she proved that she was sick by emptying the contents of her stomach into the bucket we had provided for her.

Surely she will feel better now, I tried to convince myself and my husband who I knew was really wishing that I would just give up the trip. What is the difference if she lies in the back of the van or at home on the couch? She had a good record of hitting the bucket, and I knew that we would not have to deal with any messes. With a small change in plans, I could still go along, that is if my husband was willing to sit in the van with the children while I did some quick shopping. I would then wait in the van with the children while he did his shopping. Since I only needed a few items at each place, he agreed.

Determined not to make my husband regret that he had agreed to these plans, I raced into Goodwill at our first stop. It would have been fun to look around since it was 50% off day, but there was only one thing I was really wanting to find this day. I was looking for rollerblades for the twins' birthday that was only about a week away. And there they were—only one pair and not rollerblades—but a cute pair of pink and white roller skates. In record time I made my way out to the van. All eyes were glued to my big package that was double bagged. Nobody could guess the bargain I had just found in a couple minutes.

Our second stop was at Aldi. My husband dropped me off at the entrance, and since I only needed two things, yogurt and bananas, I bypassed the carts. Just inside the door, I saw they had cabbage on sale. I had been so hungry for cabbage lately, so I delightedly grabbed two heads. I considered going back out for a cart, but I knew that would be taking more of my husband's precious time. So I headed to the back of the store. I found two containers of yogurt to be quite awkward, so I looked around for a box. With the box, I made my way to the bananas. Before arriving, I could not help but notice the grapes were a nice price too. Two 2-lb. boxes of grapes really added to the bulkiness of my burden, but I managed to add several bags of bananas to my already full load. By this time I realized that even the box I had chosen was too small! Trying to appear confident, I made my way to the checkout, wishing desperately I had taken time to grab a cart.

At the checkout, I was able to take a short break and reorganize my items. I jokingly told the cashier that I should have known better coming into Aldi without a cart, and she agreed that my comment was a familiar one.

Strategically placing the items in my arms, I made a beeline for the door. Stepping outside, I glanced over the parking lot noticing our tan van parked fairly close. I could feel the cabbage starting to slip, so I had one aim in mind—to get to the van as soon as I possibly could. As I rapidly crossed the parking lot, I heard the staccato "bomp, bomp" of a horn across the parking lot. Glancing quickly, I thought I noticed someone waving. I did not have any free hands to wave, so I gave a smile and got back to my mission.

I have a terrible time knowing one vehicle from another, but I figured my husband would know who it was that recognized me.

Just as I was getting close to the van, it started backing up. *Oh, no!* I thought. *Please don't pull out now.* I mentally willed my husband to stop because I wanted to put my things in the back of the van. As if he read my mind, he stopped. I dropped my grocery load with a heavy thud on the back fender. With a quick jerk I opened the back door and a cheery female voice rang out, "Sorry, you got the wrong vehicle." I stared with disbelief into the eyes of an entire stranger.

Suddenly, I knew what the staccato "bomping" across the parking lot meant. My husband and children were over there watching the entire scene. I apologized, collected my groceries, and headed to the other side of the parking lot.

My children were full of questions as to why I would do something like that, and my husband only grinned, shaking his head in wonder. My only consolation was that he did admit the vans looked very much alike even though the wheels were entirely different!

Several weeks later, I was again making a trip to town. This time I had an appointment to meet, but I thought I could probably do some shopping before my appointment since it was more convenient for my children's naptime schedule. At my last stop, I realized that I was running low on time. Making my way to the check-out counter, I groaned inwardly when my two year old said she had to go to the potty.

It seemed like a way out when my seven year old offered to take her. Under normal circumstances, I would not allow a seven year old, a three year old and a two year old to leave my side, but this was such a quiet Christian thrift store. At the moment it was not very busy, and I glanced around at the few Amish ladies also in line. "Sure," I said, "do you know where they are?"

She confidently led the girls across the hallway and into the restrooms. I was still waiting in line when I heard the first faint shriek, "MOM!"

It was a moment of *Did I hear right?* as I paused to hear if the sound came again. Sure enough! It was louder this time. I grabbed my baby and purse and fled toward the restrooms, ignoring the sympathetic glances I was getting from the Amish ladies who had also heard the cry this time.

I rushed into the restroom and around the corner stood my three little girls staring intently at the door that had a sign plainly stating, "This is not an exit." I too knew the feeling because more than once I had tried to exit via this closet door. The real exit had seemed to simply disappear.

At the sound of my voice, they turned, the terror still written on their faces. They looked at me as if I had dropped from the ceiling. "We thought we could not get out," they said with smiles replacing their frightened expressions.

Later my oldest daughter voiced her feelings, "I feel so dumb that I screamed like that." As I groped for the proper words to console her, she dropped a bomb. "I keep wondering which would be worse—screaming in a store or trying to get into a stranger's vehicle?"

No Flops, Please!
by Lydia Hess

Eager daughter stirred the dough;
But the chocolate cake lay low
When it baked. It rudely bit
Every tongue that tasted it.

Oops! No sugar. What disgust!
For life's recipe, I must
Not drop one ingredient.
Father make me diligent
(Lest some flop is my lament.)

Changed Mind
by Brenda Petre

The baby is screaming,
The little boys fighting;
They can't share their toys,
And oh, now they are biting!

I look at my husband and gravely declare,
"We *can't* have more children; I'm nearing despair!"

The baby is sleeping,
The boys have decided
That playing is fun
When the toys are divided.

I rock our wee darling—
My nose gets a "whiffer"
Of sweet-scented lotion
As softly I sniff her.

I smile at my husband, "Oh, could we survive,
If this were the last little baby we'd have?"

Do I Really Love It?
by Susan Kreider

It was a hot day, and I was busy working outside. My frustration was mounting as all I could think about was another day with so much to do, especially outdoor work. The garden was all caught up, so that wasn't a part of my problem. It was the rest of the yard.

We moved here last fall, a week before the first snowflakes came, so the very unkept, extremely neglected yard had soon been covered beneath a wonderful layer of sparkling white snow which hid all the ugliness so beautifully. But now the snow was nowhere to be seen, spring had come and gone, and although the yard had definitely taken on a much better appearance, it was still a challenge to keep after weeds that had been left completely to themselves for years. Stone pathways throughout the yard and perennial bed were anything but gorgeous with dandelions and other weeds growing throughout. I felt like despairing. I don't do messy yards and as much as I love working outside, this was more than I thought I could handle. Yes, we did have a lawn sprayer to pull behind a tractor, but the tractor that I needed to use had decided its days were being numbered, and only the master was able to operate that one. Since he was at work, it ruled out that option. So with a sigh, I walked to the garage and got out my little hand sprayer, just like I had done how many times before. I walked to the backyard and filled it up with water, added my Round Up, and away I went, mentally calculating that this was now my 15th gallon of Round Up I had sprayed in the last two months. Just as I was about 10 minutes from being done, great cries erupted from the house, and I knew I had better run—so much for quickly trying to finish.

I stepped inside the house, and there in front of my eyes was a whole gallon of milk gushing out all over the living room carpet. I grabbed the broken jug, which wasn't a very smart thing to do as milk was still pouring out and leaving a trail on my way outside, opened the door to the garage and promptly slipped on the wet concrete. Down I went with the leaking jug in hand and fuming inside. Sad to say, I gave my little girl the gears in no uncertain tones (which later I apologized for) for monkeying around with the milk jug on her way from the garage fridge to the kitchen. We all know how milk soon smells soaked in a carpet, so I called my husband and asked what I should do. We decided to go rent the carpet cleaner at our local grocery store and do a thorough job of cleaning it up. I washed up the linoleum and the concrete garage floor, then loaded the children into the van and went to rent the carpet cleaner.

Of course, seeing the sprayer still lying in the front yard didn't help my attitude. I was cross! Cross at my messy, stinky house; cross at all my weeds; cross at my daughter who could have prevented all this; cross at my oldest daughter who was slacking off in the house while I was outside. Just plain down cross! I had some thinking to do as we drove off to town, and decided that a good attitude makeover would definitely make the children, and of course myself, much happier. So we sang together as we drove back home, and once the mess was all cleaned up, I went back outside to finish my work.

• • • • •

Two weeks later we were cruising down the interstate enroute to my husband Kyle's folks who lived 30 hours away. It was the middle of July, and I was sure a good break from all the work at home would be a very welcome break—not just the yard work, but the normal, everyday work like laundry, cooking and cleaning. I don't usually tolerate much dirt in my house, so during the summer it always takes more effort to keep everything neat and tidy. Oh, don't get me wrong, I always enjoy summer, especially the fact that the children are home from school and we can all work together. Nonetheless, I was ready for a break. No more planning meals for three weeks. Wow, what a treat!

· · · · ·

After spending a week and a half visiting Kyle's folks, we travelled on to visit other friends and family. Some friends of ours whom we were hoping to visit were expecting, so I called her and asked if it would be overwhelming to have our family of six stop in for a few days. She assured me wholeheartedly that they would love that and it would be no problem at all. "As long as you don't mind the mess!" and then she added, "If you can handle living in a house that's not perfectly clean, just come on down!" I assured her that we wouldn't mind at all, and that I would do anything I could to help her out.

We arrived there on Friday afternoon, and together we put lunch on the table and did various jobs throughout the afternoon. During our discussion I asked her if she gets overwhelmed with all her work. They live in a big, spacious house that would take hours of cleaning each week, plus her husband is often at home during the day, so she cooks up a big meal three times a day. She had three children plus another one on the way, yet she was just such a happy lady! She looked at me with a big smile on her face and said, "I just love it! I love cooking and taking care of my children and laundry and everything! I just LOVE IT! Don't you?"

"Uhh, yes, I do too, I guess; I just get overwhelmed sometimes and then it's hard to say that I love what I'm doing." I was sure she knew what I meant, because like she had warned me, her house wasn't in the neatest, tip-top shape, but that didn't make her all grouchy. She didn't have to have everything sparkling clean in order to be a happy hostess! Neither was she apologizing all the time for how her house looked. She was loving her job as a mom and wife and wouldn't have traded it for anything. I felt very ashamed. Was I loving or simply tolerating my role? Here I thought I had to have everything just SO—a garden that was weed free, flower beds that were blooming without any weeds to ruin their looks, a spotless house, and food that was appreciated and tasty. What exactly were my motives? Was I actually doing it to impress, or was I doing it to serve my family? Was I grouchily rushing around trying to keep everything up to my standards, or was I taking the time to be a happy, loving mom to my dear children who would soon grow up? Those questions were being chased around in my brain, and I decided that no, I don't want to be a grouchy mom that doesn't take time for the precious moments of taking time for my children, even just little things like eating lunch outside or going on a walk. Neither would I totally neglect my house either because that would soon result in a grouchy husband (not to mention wife and children). But there is a happy medium. By God's grace, and with hubby's encouragement and advice, may we as busy moms all strive to find that happy medium, and love and enjoy to the utmost our calling as a mother!

Grow in Grace
by Regena L. Weaver

"But grow in grace . . ."
-2 Peter 3:18a

"But grow in grace . . ."
"How can I, Lord?"
    An earnest cry from honest heart.
"What does Peter mean, and how can I fulfill?"
The young bride doesn't know
    that through the years
        the Shepherd will be leading her
            and teaching her to grow . . .

Months glide by.
New life and love now fill her daytime hours,
    and Hubby labors, motivated by an extra joy.
Anticipation mounts as weeks move on.
This waiting time has purpose—
    Growth is needed
        within her heart and in this budding life.
Her loving hands prepare for heaven's gift.

The rocker squeaks a lullaby.
She plants a kiss upon the dimpled cheek
    and smiles into the blue-blue eyes.

"Oh Baby Dear, I love you so!
I think,
    this love I feel for you, my Tiny One,
        must be akin to that great love of His
            that moved His Father-heart to send His Son.
He loves His daughter, too,
    just as I do you!"

"Don't touch!"
A short command requires swift response.
Little fingers reach for hot taboos . . .
    a candle's dancing flame,
    a wood stove's tantalizing warmth.
To disobey brings pain.
"I understand, O Lord,
    I'm like my little girl.
        If I refuse to heed Your call
            I hurt myself, and pain Your heart, besides . . ."

"You'll need to wait
    'cause Mama's rocking little brother . . ."
She wants a cracker,
    NOW!
        but Baby can't be hurried.
(It's hard to be a lass of three
    when Mama's so hard pressed to reach around . . .
She doesn't know that sometimes Mama yearns
    for time to simply be herself.
        Not "Mom," but "Me!")

"God."
    With halting voice she tries the word.
Then "God . . . is . . . love."

She's learning words,
> and at the same time learning Bible truths.

Truths that will sink in deeper as she grows.

"God is love!"
> More confidently now.
> First grader knows the words;
> Her mother, listening, feels the truth,
>> and grows.

"Must I finish, Mama?"
> Those same blue eyes, now clouded with distaste.

"I'm sure that Karen doesn't need to work this hard!
> Besides, their stack of dishes isn't near this tall."

A golden chance
> to teach this tender mind
>> that work is meant to be enjoyed,
>>> although it isn't always fun.

A fresh reminder, for herself, as well . . .
> The mending pile is high,
>> but it's a proof of healthy brood.
> A smile and thankful heart
>> will be an aid in conquering it!

The child matures.
She sees her need of Christ, and yields.
One battle has been won,
> but others come.

She needs a mother's guidance, love and prayer
> to help her through.

"The Christian life is one of service.
> Commit it all to Him—He'll show the way."

Advice she gives to growing daughter

  is what she needs, herself,
    throughout the day.

A mother's daily call is one of service.
Contentment will be found
  in serving Jesus . . .
    Despite impatient teen's voice calling for his shirt,
      and sticky fingers clinging to their Mama's skirt.
The nest is empty.
Home is quiet, now, for hours on end.
The former bride,
  with silver garnished hair,
    moves very slow.
  No trace of bounce of yesterday.
She longs to go
  where Time no longer has control.
Yet feeble outward strength
  is overshadowed by great strength within.
That youthful prayer was heard . . .
  In intervening years
    her Father gently led,
      and nurtured growth.

And still she'll grow,
  until His call to go . . .

Mommy and the Kangaroo Car

by Lucille Martin

Last night we took our son to his first cattle auction. Wilson is four months old, so no doubt it is time to begin his education so that he'll be ready to follow in the footsteps of his farmer-at-heart daddy.

Wilson enjoyed the commotion. He sat on my lap and sucked his pacifier contentedly and watched everything happening below us. So far, so good.

Until I felt a certain vibration and decided we'd better make a trip to the car and the diaper bag. That's when the trouble began. I carried my 17-lb. baby across the parking lot to the car, only to discover that there were no more Pampers in the diaper bag. Oh no! For the first time I had forgotten, in my hurry to leave, to check the side pocket of the diaper bag. Now I was stranded without clean diapers.

Back across the parking lot and up the steps we went. I explained the problem to my husband, and told him I'd have to take Wilson home for a clean-up. He handed me the keys. "Remember the emergency brake," he reminded me. "And do you know where reverse is?"

We had just acquired this old car as an alternative to a truck, and it was a manual. I had driven it only once with my husband coaching me, but it had gone fairly well. I assumed that I could drive ten minutes home and back with only a reasonable amount of difficulty.

I strapped Wilson into his car seat and settled into the driver's seat. *Now, let's see. Release the emergency brake, and keep my foot on the brake pedal so I don't drift into the car in front of me.* I started the car, put the gearshift in reverse, and tried to back up.

Something went terribly wrong. The car made a horrible, humiliating roar, jerked backward, and stalled. The man outside the entrance whipped his head around to see what sort of monster was on the loose. Something in me was begging, *Get out of sight! Quickly!*

But the car did not cooperate. I put it in first gear and it stalled. And stalled. And stalled. After about six tries to drive away, I gave up. I was getting out of the car when one of the auction workers came up. "What's wrong with it?" he asked.

"Nothing," I replied, "but I only drove it once before."

"Are you going to be okay?" he asked next.

"I'm going in here to get my husband," I explained, preparing to get Wilson out of his seat again.

"What's his name?" the man asked. I told him, and tried to explain where he was sitting. The man disappeared inside the building, and a few minutes later my husband appeared. His expression was a combination of curiosity, amusement, and concern.

"It won't work," I half-wailed, half-laughed. "It roared and stalled, and I can't get it to go!" I had no idea what I had done wrong, but I no longer wanted to drive home. My husband kindly took the wheel and we drove home laughing. I was sure that man at the auction hadn't seen anything so funny in a week. I still felt humiliated, but at least we were out of sight, and I didn't have to reason with the car anymore.

But as soon as Wilson was changed and the diaper bag was restocked with Pampers, my husband insisted that I drive back to the auction. I reluctantly agreed because I knew I should learn, and the only way to learn was to practice.

The reverse business went slightly better after one stalled attempt. But when I tried to release the clutch and drive away, the car jumped like a kangaroo. I jumped with it. Wilson screamed. My husband looked out the side window and mumbled something unintelligible.

Nevertheless, he was not ready to give up. We went through the whole starting, bucking, stalling process again. By this time I was shaking with helpless laughter, and Wilson thought his world was coming to an end. After calming both of us down, my husband coached me again, and we made it safely onto the road. I changed gears smoothly several times, and we headed back into town. I squealed the tires a little at one stoplight, but no more disasters occurred. We reached the auction and parked with little difficulty, and I heaved a sigh of relief. My blood pressure dropped to a safer level at last.

I stayed in the car to feed the baby, and tried to relax. It was comforting to be out of sight and holding my baby. That's what mommies do best, after all. They simply aren't made for kangarooing. At least not this mommy.

Grown Up
by Becky Newswanger

He brought me his coat with a winning grin,
And grinned still more when I helped him in.
He brought his boots, and his mittens too.
I couldn't mistake what he wished to do.
So I bundled him up, and sent him out.
Of his pride and delight he left no doubt.
I knew in that moment I had let go
Of the baby boy I used to know.

My Loaves
by Becky Newswanger

O Lord, I hear the tramping of a thousand people's feet.
They are treading past our cottage on the dusty village street.
To hear Thy wisdom from Thy lips, to view Thy matchless power,
They follow Thee unwearyingly for hour after hour.

But Savior, I must stay at home, and tend our little ones.
I wish that I could hear Thee speak till setting of the sun.
I wish with Thy disciples, I could share the bread Thou'st blest,
And bring the blind and lame to Thee, the weary and depressed.

But maybe, Lord, my lot will be a basket lunch to fill,
And send a lad with ready heart to share it at Thy will.
Oh, help me pack his lunch with love, and truth and purity,
Prepare his feet to tread the path of usefulness to Thee.

I cannot feed the hungry throng, or heal the blind and lame,
But help me teach our children, Lord, the marvels of Thy name.
And when their simple basket lunch, they place within Thy hand,
I offer Thee my lowly loaves to use at Thy command.

Out-of-Hand, Into His Hand
by Lydia Hess

When your toddler's Sunday pants
Meet the creosote, when ants
Bring their whole extended family to your shelves,
When your scissors-happy tot
Shreds the roses in your pot,
While you tackle drawers that can't contain themselves;
When the barber finds his sis
And you find a tattered miss,
When the flying cup and saucer crash to land . . .
Smile at aggravation's face;
Cast your cares on God, and place
Out-of-hand affairs in His controlling hand.

Learning by Doing
by Brenda Petre

They have these schools for would-be clerks,
For doctors, sheriffs, others,
But no one's teaching basic skills
For being better mothers!

They are not teaching faster ways
(Though every mother wishes)
For scrubbing grease from boys' pants,
Or washing dirty dishes.

Nor, what to do on rainy days
With children who are hyper;
And absolutely not the knack
Of washing out a diaper!

So many schools, for many jobs
That people are pursuing,
But something hard as motherhood
We have to learn by doing!

The Measure of My Days
by L. D. Nolt

*LORD, make me to know mine end,
and the measure of my days, what it is;
that I may know how frail I am.
-PSALM 39:4*

I don't know how it is in your home, but I have a constant struggle in my life to keep things in the proper perspective. Each day follows the next and in the flurry of school, dishes, laundry, tears, cuddling, discipline, and all that goes into the rearing of children and the organization of being a wife and mother, I tend to lose my focus at times.

Sometimes all it takes is a pinprick of my conscience to make me realize how far off course I have wandered, but sometimes it takes more of a blow.

Maybe it is the death of someone I know, hurts that have to do with friends or with church issues, struggles with patience, or a soft answer. Maybe it is a word of correction given to me by a concerned friend, or a close friend suffering a health issue.

How quickly those trying times can be a stark reminder of our frailty and humanness! All of a sudden we realize that we really have no control and how much better it can be if we can stay focused on the fact that we are simply a frail man in need of continuous help from our Savior.

I often think of the words to the song, "Lord, don't move that mountain, just give me strength to climb. For if You would move each mountain I might grow weaker every time. And just as your Son Jesus, took that cross up Calvary's hill, Lord, don't move that mountain so I may ever do Your will."

I need those constant reminders to keep my perspective in the right place. Sometimes even my children have words of advice. My husband and I were discussing how nice it would be to add a small portion onto the kitchen someday in the distant future.

"We have a nice house," my husband concluded, drawing my dreaming to a close for the moment.

My daughter piped up, "Let your conversation be without covetousness; and be content with such things as ye have: for he hath said, 'I will never leave thee, nor forsake thee.'"

Her Bible verse for the week came in handy to set me back on the right track to remind me to remember the "measure of my days, that I may know how frail I am."

Carol in July
by Lydia Hess

"Joy to the world!" the children swell
    With chorus that rejoices;
The rippling heat waves cannot quell
    The luster of their voices.

They chime, "Rejoice, Emmanuel . . ."
    Year-round! Perhaps the reason:
Their mother needs to hear them tell,
    "Joy always is in season!"

These Are Our Children
by Darletta F. Martin

I will put my trust in Him . . . I and the children which God hath given me. -Heb. 2:13

Those were my children.
I was their teacher. I entered the classroom
and claimed them as mine.
Daily instruction was mine to endow them:
reading and history, science and math.
Always more work than we could accomplish;
each day all the dutiful raced with the clock.
What's most important? Who is most needy?
Multiple choices a teacher must make.
But not all alone.
They had parents who loved them, clothed them,
provided them safe, Christian homes.
Now when I see them embarking adulthood,
I know that the union of home, school and church
Directed the lives of these children to rightness,
guided their choices toward heavenly truth.
These are my children.
I am their mother. I married their daddy and took them as mine.
Daily I feed them and bathe them and clothe them,
settle their squabbles and wipe away tears.

Always more work than I can accomplish;
burdens that never existed before.
What's most important? Who is most needy?
Multiple choices a mother must make.
But not all alone.
We have Daddy who loves us.
Daddy who cares about each of his own.
Along with my ardor for teaching and training,
I know that the union of husband and wife
Must firmly be anchored with love and commitment,
working together to lead them aright.
These are our children.
Wherever we labor, teach us, O Lord, to be partners for Thee,
That mother or father or teacher or preacher,
we may lead onward with wisdom and song
And say when we enter the gateway of heaven,
"These are our children. We brought them along."

While Folding Clothes
by Lydia Hess

I bury my nose in the blanket
I fetched from the line outside;
I savor the blend of nature
Confined in the clothes that dried:
A bit of the heaven's aura,
A snatch of the sunshine's blaze . . .
The scent of the line-dried laundry
Is part of my incense—praise!

WEAK, BUT WILLING
by Lydia Hess

"Good job!" I tell my five year old
Who finished washing dishes.
The counter's crumbs seem large and bold,
The sink looks like some fishes
Left algae scum; while residue
Is clinging to the skillet.
The drainer whispers that a new
Dish-tender tried to fill it . . .
But when I praise, "Good job!", I'm not
Pretending—I'm not lying—
Because my daughter earns a lot
Of credit, just for trying.
Delightful thought: the Lord surveys
My puny expeditions;
He pardons my imperfect ways
When I have true ambitions.

God's Love
by MJZ

Tina had shown me the paper a few days ago while I was giving directions to someone else, rocking the baby, and planning supper.

"Mom, I made this for you." One of the hundreds she made for me. Dear girl. I smiled and admired it without really seeing it. "Put it on the fridge with a magnet."

And there it was this morning. The words leaped out and grabbed me. Grabbed hold of my fretting, my weariness, my rebellion at change.

Our oldest daughter had gone away to teach school. It had happened too fast. No longer were all our children safe in our nest; safe under my wing.

I know it is inevitable that our children grow up. But not yet. I wasn't ready.

And there on the fridge in typical first-grade fashion, that green paper proclaimed this simple truth.

"God loves me.
God loves Mom.
God loves Dad."

Indeed God loves us all. It is enough.

Kept Safely
by Lucille Martin

My precious son, with all his baby charms,
I know will soon—too soon—outgrow my arms.
And then, I wonder, who will soothe his heart
And comfort him when we are far apart?

But when he's grown I pray that he will be
A son of God's; for then I will rest free,
Knowing that he'll be safe from life's alarms,
For none has ever yet outgrown *God's arms.*

First Glimpse
by Lucille Martin

No fear of first impressions (though we'd never met before),
No worries (Will he like me? Will he think me quite a bore?).

I saw his perfect innocence, no polished, put-on charms;
I only knew I loved him as I took him in my arms.

He's just one tiny baby in an awesome universe,
But I will long remember when I met him for the first.

Life at Mountain Lane
by Darla Weaver

The phrase "tied to Mom's apron strings" has taken on new meaning this morning. I am inching along a row of beans, filling a bucket with ripe ones, while two-year-old Matthan is clinging to my apron strings.

He's pretending to be driving a horse, except about once every two and a half minutes, when a jet rumbles in the distance. He's terrified of those mutterings in the sky because he knows that sometimes they thunder overhead with a deafening racket. Consequently, he refuses to be separated from my apron. When he hears the high-pitched whine of another approaching jet, he forgets that I am a horse and remembers that I am a Mom—a person good for clinging to and wailing on when life frightens or insults him.

My children always were the clingy type. As toddlers they were adventurous go-getters, but only when Mom was nearby. During that stage in life just being on the opposite side of the door from me caused them to stage a melt-down, complete with loud screeching and door kicking. The thought of sending my oldest son to school almost made me break out in hives. I wasn't sure that he would survive. Me, either, of course, but that is another story.

Nor did any of them ever become attached to a fuzzy blanket that became like a tattered member of the family. They simply attached themselves to Mom instead, and she at times felt that her nerves were becoming equally frayed around the edges.

Instead of a blanket like other children have, my daughter preferred holding on to my neck when she was a toddler. If anything ever was a nuisance, that was. I had to be in close proximity whenever she needed the security of clinging to my neck.

One evening when they were settling down on my bed for our nightly story time, I was too far away. "No, no," she protested. "If you're there I can't hold your neck."

Now I have another toddler, and he's not attached to any inanimate blanket either. To go to sleep he holds my forearm, twisting and pinching the skin with two of his fingers. I normally tolerate it quite well until some unusually hard pinches will cause me to jump and protest.

I've always loved my children. But there have been times when I've wished they didn't love me quite so much.

Yet when they're not clinging to me they're often providing enough smiles and outright laughter to balance the scales in their favor. The annoyances and frustrations diminish with time, leaving me with memories to cherish.

Such as the times I notice with resignation that two heads, side by side, are thrust into the refrigerator again. One head is covered with curly, light brown hair and belongs to my busy little toddler, Matthan. The second head, quite a bit nearer to the floor, is tawny, squarish, and has pointed ears sticking upward on each side. It belongs to the cat.

Whenever Matthan opens the outside door, that spoiled cat darts inside on his silent white feet. His destination is always the refrigerator. He lurks in front of it, waiting for the door to be opened, and he purrs coaxingly. Surely this time a snack will be forthcoming.

Matthan is happy to oblige. While the cat curls insistently around his legs, he pulls open the fridge door. When the door is ajar they stand side by side, hopefully inspecting the contents. It is a picture as precious as it is annoying.

Our oldest son will celebrate birthday number twelve soon. He will receive cards and gifts and dollars and congratulations. What's he being paid and congratulated for, I wonder. Simply for the privilege of living perhaps. And I think, shouldn't I get at least a few cards too? Perhaps something like, "Congratulations on surviving the first twelve years of motherhood!" or "Surprise! You've morphed into a mom. When did it happen?"

So after all, being a mom is no joke, what with the tantrums and the whining, being thrown up on, coughed on, wet on, and sneezed at; potty training that drags on indefinitely; and disrupted sleep at all hours and at all times. A mom gets about 15 years—give or take a few—to turn a child into (hopefully) a respectable and respectful human being. It's a lot of hard work, no mistake about it.

But when it really comes right down to it, I know that the children have already richly repaid me for anything I do. I don't need any cards or gifts. I've been paid in terms of hugs and smiles and happy chatter, and more joys than I could possibly mention. I've been paid with all the love and light and laughter with which they've filled our log home here in the hills.

Because in spite of days that bring one turmoil after another, there's nothing—not writer or homemaker or gardener or secretary or career woman of any sort—that I'd rather be than a mom.

And if they needed me to, I'd do every minute of it all over again.

The Potty Train
by Rebecca Newswanger

Toot! Toot! Click! Clack!
Get off the track!
The potty train is coming back!

My mommy is the engineer,
And though I like to help her steer,
To me the signals don't seem clear.

But you should hear the whistle blow
When Mommy says, "It's time to go."
I wonder . . . but she seems to know.

Sometimes she whispers, "We're too late.
Oh, Benjie, you must learn to wait."
That's hard for me to contemplate.

When I grow up to be a man
Like Dad and Jay and Uncle Dan,
I'll drive a train. I think I can:

But here and now I want it plain,
It won't be just a potty train.

A Garden for the Children
by Darla Weaver

Some of my earliest memories center around my mother's huge vegetable garden. Whether we children were helping to pick the produce, merely digging holes in the rich, dark soil, or seated on the cool porch shelling mountains of peas, summertime memories were made outdoors among the gardens and the flowers. Along the way we also learned valuable lessons about work ethics, finishing a job we started, sharing, helping each other, and growing our own food.

Many of the things we learned as children I want to pass on to my own children. And what better place to begin than in the garden?

Cody was six when he first asked for his own garden. "I wish I had a place to grow things," he said.

"Me too," Alisha chimed in. She was four.

I found a small plot of ground, sandwiched between the swing in my flower garden and my raised herb bed, which seemed suitable for them. I divided it into two parts, gave them each a packet of nasturtium seeds, and showed them how to dig a hole and insert a seed. That entertained them for a while.

It was spring, and I was also busy planting flower and vegetable starts from my parents' greenhouses. Whenever I brought home another tray of plants, Cody would help himself to several. Soon their little gardens were full of a hodge-podge of plants.

Next I helped them make a small wooden sign for their gardens. "Cody's Garden" read the one we pounded into the soil near his space. "Alisha's Garden" said the other one.

Those gardens started out the same, but their fate was quite different. Around Cody's garden sign nasturtiums grew thickly and flourished with vivid flowers. However, the tiny green seedlings in the adjoining garden didn't seem to thrive. One day they disappeared entirely. This puzzled me considerably, and I asked Alisha about it.

"I pulled them out," she explained. "I was tired of them."

In the same way she tired of the remaining plants and eliminated them until only a bare patch of brown soil surrounded the "Alisha's Garden" sign, and greatly amused me and everyone else who chanced to see it.

More seasons winged past. Spring came once more and the children wanted gardens again. Again they planted in their own spaces behind the swing. One short year had turned Alisha into a gardener. This summer she didn't pull out her flowers. Quite to the contrary, she dug out many of mine to transplant to her garden!

My favorite memory of my little girl from last summer is seeing her crouched in her flowerbed, busily digging a hole for the latest flower she had acquired. She had invaded my bed of cosmos and dug out one that was almost as tall as herself. "Alisha, that will never grow," I told her. But it did, and bloomed cheerfully in her garden all summer and fall.

Then winter came, and we stayed indoors and dreamed of next summer's gardens. One day I overheard the children discussing what they wanted to plant in their little gardens the following year. "I want corn and peas and potatoes and pumpkins," said Cody, and I knew they had outgrown the tiny spaces behind the swing.

One day we went outside and found a larger space just beyond my vegetable garden. We put some crude wooden markers in each of the four corners and applied a heavy kill-mulch to the existing grass. We ordered some bush cherries to plant along the back, and they will have fun deciding what else they want to plant in their new, larger garden.

Now another generation of children is learning how to dig and plant, how to care for the soil, and how to grow and harvest their own food. Along the way I hope they will learn many other valuable lessons.

I am reminded of the old Spanish proverb: "More in the garden grows / than what the gardener sows."

My Race
by Becky Newswanger

There are letters to mail, and bills to be paid;
Dishes to wash, and bread to be made;
Laundry to fold, the baby to rock.
My instinct forbids a look at the clock.

The dishwater's run, so I dash for a stamp,
And pause on the way to dust off a lamp.
I settle a quarrel, and pick up a shoe . . .
Now tell me, what was it I wanted to do?

I expect if I'd learn to stick to a chore,
And finish it up before I start more,
I'd find that my life is much less of a race,
And I'd learn to enjoy a far steadier pace.

Surrogate Mother
by Darletta Martin

I was a teacher for 16 years. I loved being a teacher. It was a noble job and fulfilling. Children loved and obeyed me. Parents thanked me for doing my job well. I didn't mind teaching the 5000th class, filling out the 640th report card, or putting up the 80th bulletin board, because I loved the people I was serving.

But I was told repeatedly—by those who know—about the "Greater Calling." Motherhood. The ultimate responsibility. The truest sense of fulfillment. In my more leisurely moments, I felt a twinge of regret that I was missing this wonderful opportunity.

Now God has called me to be a mother. But it is not glorious. It is not noble. It is piles of laundry, crumby floors, grimy walls, and hours of food preparation. It is bitter complaining, angry fights, and disobedient children. It is sorrow and toil and frustration.

I know why. I am only a pretend mother. A substitute. A servant who does the dirty work. I did not experience the poignancy of bringing these children into the world. I became their mother because their birth mother could not care for them, their adoptive mother received an early invitation to glory, and their daddy chose me to fill the void. They do not love me. They do not want me. They do not obey me. Why should they? I am not a good mother. I have had less than one year of experience.

Maybe that's the problem. I remember my first year of teaching. It was piles of papers, crumby grades, pitiful classes, and hours of lesson preparation. It was bitter complaining, sloppy work, and disobedient children. It was sorrow and toil and frustration.

I felt like a pretend teacher. I didn't know how to enforce rules. The children didn't respect me as an authority figure. I was their teacher only because the former teacher had quit, and the board couldn't find anybody else who would accept the job.

Year by year, I learned. Effort . . . patience . . . discipline . . . love . . . experience. At last I became a real teacher. I felt like a real teacher. The children knew I was a real teacher. I was *their* teacher, and they did not want to part with me. We had a delightful relationship.

So maybe 16 years from now, after the 23,000th load of laundry, the 18,000th meal, and the 900th floor washing, I will have learned. Effort . . . patience . . . discipline . . . love . . . experience. I will be a real mother. I will feel like a real mother. My children will say I am *their* mother. We will have a delightful relationship. Is that too much to hope for?

So help me, Lord.

One year later...

Surmounting Mom
by Darletta F. Martin

Almost two years have passed since I became a mother. We've been through some grueling experiences—my husband and children and I. I didn't feel like a real mother at first, and my children knew it. I couldn't love and discipline them as a real mother should, because we hadn't bonded yet. Consequently, they didn't think I merited much respect or obedience.

But I think I'm learning. My life revolves around my children now. We enjoy working together. I miss them when we are separated. And their troubles trouble me according to the Scriptural prophecy: *Yea, a sword shall pierce through thy own soul also.*

After a difficult year, my husband and children and I decided to send our emotionally-disturbed daughter to a residential treatment center halfway across the continent. Of all the options we considered, this one seemed most likely to be effective, since it was designed for her specific type of need. We drove her there—a 14-hour trip during which she expressed her anxiety in extreme ways. With relief, we deposited her into the care of capable staff members. Yet I found myself crying as we said goodbye and left her there. I saw tears in my husband's eyes too, but my turmoil of feeling felt too weighty to express even to my closest confidant. Did I love her after all? I had feared that I didn't.

Back home again, I focused on giving our young sons all the attention they had been lacking while we struggled with their sister's issues. With joy, I watched our middle child blossom into a more obedient and dutiful boy. When I showed interest in his stone collecting and school day rehearsals, he became willing to walk along to the pasture to fetch cows. He started volunteering to stay and help me with milking or housework when his daddy got called away to help others. Some physical infirmities, including poor eating habits, are fading into oblivion. He and I have discovered our need of each other. He is my son, and I am his mother.

But my youngest child continued to struggle with opening his heart all the way. He preferred the security of his daddy's care. Sometimes he demanded my attention to his needs but showed no obligation to respect my decisions. Buried grief and anxiety still boiled into frustration and anger on the surface of his life. The intensity of his issues threatened my connections with him.

One evening shortly before we planned to visit our daughter for the first time since her placement, my husband needed to be away at a late-night meeting. I wanted to put our boys to bed, but Younger Son refused to cooperate. I could see that he wasn't planning to sleep until Daddy came. Instead he kept disturbing and scaring his brother. Suddenly I realized that he must be afraid. Harshness and punishment would not avail.

In an attempt to calm both of us, I took him to the kitchen table. We sat and colored together in his John Deere coloring book for almost an hour. Finally he admitted to being tired. I offered that he could leave his bedroom door open, and I would leave mine open until Daddy came home. He agreed and went to sleep peacefully. I hoped he knew how much I loved him.

I worried about going on a two-day trip, leaving a scared, forsaken boy at home. We discussed the issue until Younger Son expressed satisfaction with the idea of his married brother and sister-in-law sleeping here at our house, so he could have his own bed. We called the boys several times during our trip, and Younger Son always answered the phone. He didn't talk long, but he always sounded content. When we returned, he came running out the lane to meet us. I opened the truck door and scooped him in with me, and he wriggled with delight. He went wild with exuberance when he pulled the toy airplane I had brought for him out of my bag.

After a happy evening together, I was afraid he wouldn't settle down to sleep. I suggested that Daddy help him get ready for bed, but he wanted to talk to me. So we talked until he snuggled into bed with a book to read for a few minutes before he fell asleep. He's my little boy, and he needs me. Together we learn important lessons.

Our struggles aren't over yet, I know. We have mountains enough to challenge us for months and years yet. But I am their mother. They are my children. We love each other, and God is helping us as we climb.

STRAIGHT TO MY FATHER
by MJZ

I was coming in from the nursery with Baby in my arms and two-year-old Kathy following me. Daddy was preaching. I turned into our bench and sat down, adjusting the sleeping baby, and only then noticed that Kathy had not turned in after me!

She was headed up the center aisle with only one goal in mind—Daddy.

Am I so focused on my Heavenly Father? Yearning to be with Him, reaching and moving ever closer to Him. Not distracted by anything around me.

He is waiting with open arms. My Father. And when I am safe in His arms He will not gently turn me around and whisper in my ear, "Go to Big Sister."

Through a Glass, Darkly
by Darletta F. Martin

Charity suffers long . . .
But I am tired of waiting.
My children ought to know
The ways in which to grow
And when to stop their fighting.
They ought to stay alert
And focus on their work
And answer when I'm calling.

Lord, help me to remember:
They think as children do.
I once was childish too,
With actions quite appalling.
I'll love them while I wait.
When they become adult
And think the way they ought,
My love will be too late.

LOVE NOTE
by Darletta F. Martin

Our youngest son has learned to write
    And thoroughly enjoys it.
We find the budding sentences
    That show how he employs it.

My mother died, his pencil cries.
    And she is safe in heaven.
He writes the grief he cannot speak—
    This boy who just turned seven.

He struggles still to place his heart
    Securely in my keeping;
It's hard to heed another mom
    Before he's finished weeping.

But when I put his clothes away
    I find a letter saying,
*Dear Mom I like you very much
And you like me. Love Dalen.*

He feels his new mom's love for him
    And wants, in turn, to bless her.
His words will stand for many years;
    He wrote them on his dresser!

When He Can't Find the Pocket
by Darletta F. Martin

Michael wanted to make a house. He had a cardboard water heater box and a vision. When he found me in the milking parlor, he asked, "Mom, where's a knife I can use to cut my door and windows?"

"Get that old, dull, paring knife out of my gray hooded sweater pocket," I said.

"I'm afraid I won't be able to find it."

"Yes, you can. I know that knife is in the pocket of my gray sweater. It's hanging on the right side of the closet, right next to my heavy brown sweater. I just used that knife for some garden work yesterday."

"I wish you would get it for me."

"No, I'm milking." Surely a nine year old could go to the house and fetch his own knife.

Within five minutes, Michael reappeared in the doorway, wearing a persecuted look. "I can't find it."

"What do you mean? You can't find my sweater?"

"No, I found both of your gray sweaters, but it's not there."

"The knife isn't in the pocket? I'm sure it is. I just wore that sweater this morning."

"I can't . . ." Michael looked ready to cry, ". . . find the pocket."

I almost laughed. Wasn't my son putting forth any effort to help himself? "You can't find the pocket? Well, pull the sweater off the hook. You can't hurt it."

"Michael," my husband called from the front of the parlor, "I need you to open the barnyard gate. I want to walk this lame heifer around by the driveway to put her back in the box stall."

Michael went. While they put the heifer in her pen and I chased another row of cows into the parlor, I analyzed Michael's problem. He seemed seriously befuddled. Why couldn't he find my sweater pocket? I had given him explicit directions. Was his listening comprehension so deficient?

Suddenly something clicked. He said he saw two gray sweaters . . . No pockets . . .

"Michael!" I called out the window of the holding area.

He looked up from chaining the barnyard gate. "What?"

"Which closet did you look in? The Sunday one or the barn one?"

"Sunday."

"So you checked my Sunday sweater and my knockabout sweater?"

He nodded.

I laughed lightly. "That's just what I suddenly thought you must have done. No wonder you couldn't find a pocket; those sweaters don't have any pockets! I was talking about the gray *hooded* sweater I wear to the barn. It's in the *barn* coat closet."

"Oh!" Michael laughed now too. "I didn't know you meant that." He took off running for the house. The next time he saw me in the holding area, he shouted from the sandbox, "Mom! I got my door and one window cut. I'm taking a break now before I cut another one."

He was happy with his house. I was happy with my success in figuring out his problem. How often, in both greater and lesser matters than this, I need to slip inside my child's mind before scolding him for not being able to accomplish what seems so simple. Maybe we haven't both been looking in the same closet. God forbid that I belittle my son for failing to find a pocket that isn't there.

Of Pacifiers and Prayer
by Lucille Martin

Daddy was sick in bed. Wilson was sick and supposed to be in bed. Mommy was sick and wished she was in bed.

Last night was just short of a living nightmare for this mommy. Caring for my very sick husband and my getting-better-but-still-sick son while I felt less than well myself had left me weak and desperate for some sleep. Not to mention that I'd already had several shattered nights.

But last evening . . . there was no pacifier. I have always been glad that Wilson liked his pacifier. He has (or, rather, had) two bright-colored ones for daily use, plus a nice blue one that stayed in the Sunday pocketbook. A week or so ago, I dug out that nice blue one for everyday because I couldn't find any others. But last evening—you guessed it—the blue one disappeared too.

I wanted nothing more than to pop a pacifier in Wilson's mouth, plop him in his bed, and collapse into mine. But first we had to find a pacifier.

I looked in all the usual places—on the high chair, on the changing table, on the kitchen counter, under the recliner, on the end stand, in Wilson's bed. No pacifier. When I crouched down to peer under the sofa, my almost-nine-month-old pulled up and leaned on me. I was already feeling very leaned-on, had been all day in fact, but I didn't have time to dwell on this thought.

I headed for Wilson's room for a more thorough search. I

pulled his mattress up so I could check beneath it. I leaned down to check the shadows under the crib. Then I lay flat on my stomach and strained to see under the cedar chest. No pacifier. When I got up, Wilson was sitting behind me, grinning. Clearly he was enjoying the show. Had I been feeling less tired, less weepy, and less ill, I might have laughed too.

Instead, I was praying. When I am desperate my prayers are not long or eloquent. "Dear God, please let me find one pacifier." That was about the extent of it. But I believed that God would hear a desperate mother's plea. Soon. After all, I was only asking for one pacifier, not all three.

At last I gave up. To my surprise, Wilson went to sleep without a struggle, and I deposited him in his bed. At long last, with my son asleep and my husband provided with pills, ice, Sprite, blankets, and what comfort I could offer, I had a moment for myself. With what little energy I had left, I showered and washed my hair.

I drifted off to sleep, hoping it would last at least a few hours without interruption. Going by the previous nights, I expected to be up and down caring for one or another of us. Sometime in a moment of half-awareness I heard Wilson cry out and pulled him into bed with me to nurse. The next thing I knew, my husband was shaking me awake. I assumed it was 3 a.m. and time for his medicine. To my amazement, he told me it was actually closer to 6:00, and I had slept practically undisturbed all that time.

With some decent sleep, my morale level had come up considerably. Especially when Wilson and I finally got up sometime after 8:30 and discovered that Daddy had recovered tremendously. That was definitely an answer to prayer.

But what about the other prayer—the missing pacifier prayer? I made several more futile searches throughout the day, and Daddy did a little checking around himself. At bedtime I resigned myself to another night without a pacifier.

Wilson had other plans. He refused to settle down. So another desperate search began. We almost turned the house upside down and shook it. I was pretty sure that Wilson had dragged that pacifier to wherever it was, because I knew where I had seen it last. We looked in reasonable places and not-so-reasonable places, and racked our brains to think of places where a baby could hide a pacifier. Wilson followed along behind, watching us stress ourselves, and unable to help.

At long, long last, Daddy got out his flashlight and attacked the Mommy-chair. It's a big stuffed recliner where Wilson and I have rocked since the day we brought him home. I had already stuck my hand down the cracks between the cushions, and found nothing. Actually, I had found a pair of Wilson's socks, but no pacifier. But when Daddy got out his flashlight, I dared to hope. Maybe, just maybe . . . Wilson and I watched as he pulled the cushions apart as far as he could and shone his light in the crack. When I saw a flash of bright green, I knew we had struck gold.

Daddy produced one everyday pacifier, and then a crochet hook that had vanished long ago. "I'm going to laugh if you find all three pacifiers in there," I told him as he continued the search. In the following three minutes he unearthed not one, not three, but a total of four pacifiers, including one we had used only briefly when Wilson was little because he didn't like it.

I didn't know whether to laugh or cry. All those hours I had spent in the Mommy-chair, and those pacifiers were so close the whole time. The answer to the desperate prayer of a sick and weary mommy. When I tucked Wilson into bed, there was a pacifier in his mouth, and a tremendous sense of relief and gratitude in the heart of his Mommy.

On Moving
by Brenda Petre

After several days of not feeling well, our two year old was moping at the breakfast table. Nothing looked good to him, and he refused every bite we offered. I was feeling desperate to get something into him before he got dehydrated.

"I know what his problem is," suggested an older sibling. "He wants to move!"

Indeed! What an easy fix!

But don't we all know the feeling? We've been sick and weary for several weeks. The housework is so far behind we start to feel like it's hopeless. What if we could just walk out on the mess and start over somewhere else?

We all know that option is unrealistic. So we beg for the daily strength to keep on—step by difficult step.

Most times there are brighter days ahead for us. But sometimes it seems like a *long* time until physical or emotional health can be restored.

Someday, and we know not which bright or stormy, cheerful or wearisome day it will be, our time to dwell here will be over. The wonderful solution to our earthly illnesses will be reached.

We can move!

BOUNCING IS BETTER
by Darletta Martin

"Life is not about how fast you run or how high you jump, but how well you bounce." My bounciest student wrote this in my autograph book just before the call to marriage halted my teaching career. *I've done all three to manage a multi-grade classroom,* I thought. *Most likely this new life won't be much different.*

But marriage brought out the real meaning of this quote. The instant I became Delmer's wife, I also became *Mom*—Mom to three children who bounced nonstop and sometimes off the wall. Needier than I had ever imagined, they expressed their needs by shouting my name whenever I left their sight. I began to run to meet their demands.

My mom had taught me how to be a running mother. Get up early, hang out all your wash, fix full-course meals, manage a large garden, fill your basement freezers for the winter, sew your children's clothes, help your husband farm, and don't take a nap unless it's absolutely necessary.

I ran as hard as I could that first summer, but it was like a bad dream—I could never find my way out of that maze of work. The faster I tried to run, the more obstacles I met. Resistant children. Shattered schedules. Lack of rest. Overwhelming stress.

For years my teachers and fellow workers had challenged me to set high goals for myself, goals that I had continually jumped to reach. Now I jumped into a role I had never filled, into a house that wasn't mine, into a family that wasn't trained according to my specs. Reaching my goals for perfection looked as impossible as touching the moon.

And that's when bouncing became necessary. All my running and jumping simply stressed me out until I learned to bounce. Bounce away from all the non-moral rights and wrongs that dominated my thought patterns. Bounce away from fearing what my family would think if I deviated from their code of ethics. Bounce away from important work to meet the more important needs of my children. Bounce away from the drive to perfect my children in the sight of others.

For instance, I came from a plan-ahead, be-ready-on-time, never-make-anyone-wait household. My new family had learned long ago that planning ahead was almost impossible, due to all the physical and emotional health problems involved. They didn't sweat if someone was still in the bathtub five minutes before we should be driving out the lane. I had to learn to bounce out of stress mode at such times and collect pieces that would be forgotten in the last-minute dash out the door.

The first time I canned peaches, I felt frantic about the huge job looming ahead. Determined to get an early start, I rushed through the barn chores until Delmer kindly told me I could go in and start my housework. When the children woke, I was in the basement peeling peaches 100 mph. They shouted for me, and I shouted back. Of course, they wanted me to come up and give them personal good-morning attention, which I refused, insisting that they join my marathon instead. All this running and jumping wore me out before breakfast. Such experiences taught me to bounce into my children's lives and get them off to a happy start before extending a hearty welcome to run in my race.

Before the summer ended, our six-year-old Dalen unintentionally gave me a beautiful bouncing lesson. One evening after milking, he and Michael went with Delmer in the rusty red dump truck to get a load of silage. There are no seat belts in the ancient rattletrap, and the doors do not latch well, but it serves its purpose around our family's farm. On the way back, the boys asked Delmer to use the Jake brake when they turned in the end of the road. As he complied, the door flew open and Dalen tumbled out onto the road. By the time Delmer got the truck stopped, Michael was leaping out the open door to see if his brother was okay. Dalen, who could have howled with injury and offense, bounced up, ready to go. At home, he told the story dramatically, showed me his brush burns, and added, "While I was rolling, I looked up and saw Michael jumping straight out of the truck. He looked like an airplane!"

No loud laments, no guilt trips, no blame on anyone else, just a story laughingly told. No self-pity, no anger at the vehicle of his pain, no fear of riding again, just a learning experience. And a good bouncing lesson for his mom.

List, Revised
by Lydia Hess

My waist-high list of: burn the trash,
Reorganize the attic's stash,
Mend trousers, fill the cookie tin,
Make sure the laundry's gathered in . . .
Can muffle holy whispers of
Some better plans of selfless love.
I'll add, "Consider" to my list,
Lest some more urgent task be missed.

LET IT SHINE
by Faith Sommers

Why don't the children hurry?

We have laundry to hang, floors to sweep, lunches to pack, dishes to wash.

But they just dawdle . . . rubbing sleep from their eyes.

Why can't they keep moving? Soon they'll leave for school, and the unfinished work is still here. All mine.

I run to the washline. I will hang out the clothes so that I don't have to watch them slowly looking for shoes and thinking about washing dishes.

As I pin tiny socks, I begin singing. The first notes that leave my lips are words of a song our toddlers are learning.

"This little light of mine, I'm gonna let it shine . . ."

Suddenly tears flow from my struggling heart and reach my eyes. My light . . . definitely not shining!

Quickly I run to the house, determined to show the children my love—and my light—before they leave for the day. Forgiving, they flash smiles, pat my hand, and race for the arriving bus.

"Won't let Satan blow it out; I'm gonna let it shine . . . Let it shine, let it shine, let it shine."

Holding the Baby
by Laura Yoder

There have been nine of them,
Each one sweeter than the one before.

There is much dirt and noise
And crying and laughing and toys.
There are many shoes and hats
And cookies and games and bats.

When they are older, there is more.
More of everything, and it is
Far deeper.
More urgent. It is life and death.
It is day and night.

So sometimes I just sit and hold
The Baby.

It is quiet, just her and I.
She is clean and smells of powder.
She is quiet, her mouth quirking
In sleepy smiles.

I hold her and it is holding
a part of me, us, and God.
It is sacred. It is love.
Pure Love.

Company Coming
by Marcia Fox

The family is waiting all out in the van,
While I give my checklist a last hurried scan.
"Set table, get butter, check crock pot," and such . . .
For company's coming to our house for lunch!
What must be in order, alas, is too much:
The table's not set, and the butter's not out,
The drain board still stands with its load all about;
The dishcloths smell sour, the towel's on the floor—
But . . .

The family is waiting! I fly out the door;
Apologize breathlessly all out the lane,
And Hubby just smiles and doesn't complain.
My mind races forward to what must be done.
I turn in my seat and address my dear Hon:
"If it can be managed," (he knows I don't tease)
"To leave church right quickly would put me at ease."
"Why, sure," he replies, very willing to please.
He knows that with makers of company lunch,
The strong, peaceful husbands stay out of the crunch!

We come to the church house and are richly fed
The spiritual banquet, by those Spirit led.
Between songs and prayers my mind wants to run
To crock pots and such 'til the service is done.
"That was a rich message," dear Betty affirms;

"We need those reminders," I say in return.
We then speak of babies (how to help them sleep)
And how to help children who too often weep.
Then Marian comes round with an interesting plan:
"Let's all get together and see if we can
Surprise your aunt Norma on Wednesday this week
Because she'll be sixty." As I hear her speak
A tussle of toddlers attracts my stern gaze;
My three-year-old son's in the thick of the maze.
I pull him up quickly from off of the floor;
Then . . .

"Mom! Dad's been waiting, and drove to the door!"
My nine-year-old daughter says quite urgently.
"You say he is waiting?!" Just how can this be,
That I who was worried about company lunch
And told my dear husband with a bit of "punch"
An early departure would help in the crunch . . .
How could I forget in the after-church talk,
My dishcloths and drain board and meat in the crock
And butter still frozen and towel on the floor?
But . . .

The family is waiting! I fly out the door.
Apologize breathlessly all out the lane,
And Hubby just smiles and doesn't complain.

Twin Song
written by a mother of ten-month-old twin boys

We're the parents of twins,
An adventure begun;
It's double the blessings—
A song often sung.

It's double the Pampers
The small hats and bibs,
The lotions and notions.
It's double the cribs.

It's double soft blankets,
The sleepers so new,
Adorable outfits,
And socks—not a few.

It's double the soft heads
And bright eyes so clear;
It's double the giggles
And smiles full of cheer.

It's double the chorus
That we hear at night;
It's double the hours
Till they're snuggled tight.

It's double the small hands
That curl round your thumb;
Two pert, little noses,
Those dear, toothless gums.

It's double the bottles
And formula cans,
Those cute pacifiers—
Toys for busy hands.

It's double the flu bugs
And hospital bills.
It's double the worry
When babies are ill.

It's double the laundry
Collecting each day;
They can get so dirty—
Those babies at play!

It's double the small mouths
That holler to eat.
It's double the high chairs;
The mess can't be beat!

It's double the sharp teeth
That bite with such skill,
The small sturdy legs
That rarely are still.

It's a double stroller
And car seats by two,
And when Mom goes shopping
There is quite a crew.

It's double the blessings
And double the joys;
It's double the trouble,
And double the noise!

Oh, we are so thankful
God blessed us this way.
May He give us strength
For the day after day!

One Mother
by MJZ

Five thousand gathered there,
And yet they all were fed,
By that one morsel-meal
Two fish, five loaves of bread.

One mother struggles here
Thronged by a multitude.
Bless me! Dear Hands Who blessed
And broke that bit of food.

I cannot reach around
Alone. But with Thy touch—
Thy hands can bless and make
One mother into much.

No Name for the Baby
by Lynette Rhodes

"Richard? Royal? Roger?" My fingers ran down the pages of the baby name book. Allen was comfortably snoozing in the recliner beside me, giving a foggy grunt to each suggestion, which I had no idea whether to interpret as approval or disapproval. "How about Robert? That's such a good, solid name—"

A gentle snore was Allen's energetic response to my consuming obsession of finding the perfect handle for the new bundle of love we were so eagerly anticipating. Our hopes and dreams had just been confirmed. Nolan was already three years old so we were absolutely thrilled to learn that God had once more visited us with the promise of life. Picking out a name was one of the most exciting duties of impending parenthood, and I could never fathom those who waited until enroute to the hospital—or even later—to settle on names. I needed to be able to whisper that Name in my heart the entire nine months of dreaming and waiting. Therefore, the pregnancy test was followed by baby name books, church directories, telephone lists, and newspapers. I was a meticulous planner, whereas hubby would have been fine with waiting until he met his new offspring to match it with a name.

Reluctantly I laid aside the books and turned my attention to Nolan, who was busy with his tractors and farm animals. We were deeply involved in herding cows into the barn when Allen startled me by popping out of his slumber with a, "Honey! I've got it! If we have a girl, let's name her Joanne."

How pleased I was to actually have an intelligent discussion on this important subject! "Joanne? That's perfect, especially since your grandmother's name is Joanna." My heart warmed with fond memories of the dear white-haired lady confined to a wheelchair but always an inspiration of cheer and gladness. She would be pleased with a namesake. My mind began spinning in the direction of fuzzy pink sleepers, dolls, and little girl ponytails. We had a son, and somehow I was picturing another li'l fellow, but a girl would be great, too. Now to come up with a good middle name . . . By this time Allen was headed out the door with Nolan in tow, for one last check in the barn. The idea of fresh air appealed to me, and I needed some alone time to ponder this nameless baby-in-making, so I quickly slipped into an old pair of shoes and headed for the back field lane. The beauty of a spring evening cannot be described, especially in light of a Creator of nature and babies alike. My heart felt so in tune with God, marveling anew at the mystery of life that God had privileged me to be a part of.

"Joanne Marie, Joanne Beth, Joanne Sue . . ." I thought of my friends, acquaintances, relatives, and like a flash it came to me—Joanne Elaine, in honor of Allen's oldest sister whose godly example had often inspired my life. Quickly I retraced my steps and met Allen just turning off the barn lights. "Guess what! I've landed on a name for a girl!" Reverently I breathed the news and saw the happy light on Allen's face as he gave his blessing upon the choice. Together we headed for the house, Nolan perched on Daddy's shoulders. By the time Nolan was tucked into bed we had agreed on a boy's name as well, and this tired mom picked up her daily journal and wrote: "Michael Lee or Joanne Elaine, we can't wait to meet you and get acquainted . . ."

Summer days came and went and then we received the joyful news of a new baby born to our closest neighbors and friends. But I gulped when the baby's name reached my ears—JOANNE! I hung up the telephone as fast as I politely could, and raced (or waddled?) out to the barn to tell Allen of this latest catastrophe. "What's wrong?" he called in alarm when he saw the look on my face.

"You wouldn't . . . believe . . . what happened," came my distressed reply between huffs and puffs. "David and Bethany . . . have a baby . . . and her name is *Joanne*," I wailed.

A puzzled look crossed my husband's face. "Is the baby okay? Or whatever is the problem?"

For a brief moment I wanted to shake him. Or box his ears. Or something. Was he actually that clueless? How could he possibly have forgotten?

"You know, that's the name we picked for our baby," I sputtered, feeling somewhat foolish for how childish it sounded.

"What name—Joanne?" he questioned.

Then I really wanted to shake him *and* box his ears. This was important to me! The life of our new family member was at stake! Well, maybe not quite, but the name of our baby was not simply a passing fancy, a like-it-or-leave-it whim. Each new little soft garment or blanket seemed to have the chosen names etched across them in letters of gold. I had doodled on scraps of paper, trying out capital and small letters, in cursive or print, in blue and pink.

Now my greatest desire is to be a godly Christian wife. And to be forbearing with my husband's shortcomings. Months later, I could laugh about this, but not now. Oh, no. At the moment, Allen could have brought me breakfast in bed, given a back rub, and presented me with a dozen red roses and I would have scorned it all. Yes, I knew I was behaving most immaturely, but . . .

We didn't speak of it again, and for the rest of the day, Allen bore a bewildered look on his face, while I fumed silently. How was I to handle this? By now I'd been married long enough to know there is no changing your man. I had visions of our baby's arrival and Allen would say, "Let's see, what did you decide to name this baby?" or "Hey, what's the name again? I keep forgetting."

Surely there was some way of searing this baby's name into my husband's brain! Somewhere that he would look at it a hundred times, but still safe from the rest of the world. But how? At last I hit upon an idea, not a very good one, to be sure, but it was the best I could come up with. I took Allen's old Bible, the one he used only for his personal devotions, and made two neat labels to paste on its vinyl cover. When I was finished, his Bible looked like this:

There! He would see it first thing every morning; then he could think about it all day long. How to get the feed bill paid, caring for a sick calf, helping his neighbor with harvesting—those were all non-issues. Carefully I laid the Bible back into the nightstand drawer.

For all my fussing, it was amazing that by the next day I'd forgotten all about this Great Plan, so when Allen shut off his alarm clock, switched on the lamp, and retrieved his Bible, I missed the look of surprise that crossed his face when he did a double take at the decorations on the cover. But his hearty chuckle fully awakened me, and he leaned over and kissed me with promises to sharpen his brains if it meant so much to me. No doubt he was fearfully envisioning where the names might pop up next if he failed this Plan. Allen assured me that he certainly did anticipate our new addition and wanted to be involved with the preparations and plans. Together we knelt to pray and another busy day began.

• • • • •

The glorious moment of triumph had come, a dark midnight hour when all heaven and earth seemed to hold its breath, and then—oh joy! Glad, wonderful joy! A new little soul is ushered into the world, and Mommy and Daddy get their first glimpse of their long-awaited gift of love.

It's a boy! He looked like a little old shriveled-up man with a hearty, angry cry, as the nurse wrapped him in a blanket and placed him in my outstretched arms. Allen and I planted kisses all over his downy-soft cheeks, unaware of anything or anyone else but this wonderful new son.

Our dear old family doctor smiled down upon us, and then, oh, so innocently asked, "What's his name?"

And that husband of mine—how I loved him at the moment! In a voice reverent with fatherly pride, he drew a deep breath and said: "Michael Lee."

And I was supremely content.

THE MOTHER MENDER
by Author Unknown

I came apart at the seams yesterday,
Children crying—
Supper frying—
Husband sighing—
But last night I knelt to pray,
And Jesus took the tensions all away.

Today the same old seams were frayed.
Weather dreary,
Children teary,
Husband weary,
But God's peace was underlaid,
And I was strong because I prayed.

BEWILDERED
by Jodi Wise

I stand bewildered, Lord—
    Dazed
at the rate our family has grown
from the size of two and four
    yesterday—
a short (and long) sixteen years
    ago—
to the thirteen it is today.

I stand bewildered, Lord—
    Perplexed,
tempted to question why
You've given me
scatter-brained tendencies,
a lack of noticing details,
an urge to write—
and eleven children;
While at the same time
You've given
my sister-in-the-faith
precise and orderly ways,
boundless energy,
yearning, empty arms—
and a stillborn son.

I stand bewildered, Lord—
    Stunned
at the speed each child
outgrows his wardrobe;
at the amount of food
teenage sons inhale each day;
at the rate the laundry mountains
mushroom
during the night.

I stand bewildered, Lord—
    Lost
in a forest of Should-Be-Dones,
trying vainly to differentiate
the Nows from the Soons,
and the Soons from the Laters.
Despair lurks and chortles
in the shadows,
knowing any Soons and Laters
will only be found deep
in the adjoining forest
of Not Enough Time.

I stand bewildered, Lord—
    Weary

of refereeing squabbles and spats,
never quite knowing
who is in the wrong
or the right;
of searching for the black holes
that aspirated
the last functioning pen,
the missing puzzle piece,
and the last matching sock;
of managing the chore-persons
who would rather
dawdle and pout,
or tussle and giggle
than fulfill their mother's dream
of seeing the work fly.

I stand bewildered, Lord—
    Amazed
that any one person could make
so many mistakes,
and that You are merciful
enough
to forgive them all;
that You are gracious enough
to provide the strength to face
the next week
or day
    or hour
        or . . .
            moment.
I stand bewildered, Lord—
    Awed,
speechless,
to see our oldest ones
become
newborn sons of God
in spite of us,
their very human parents.

And I dream of the day
I will stand before You
    Carefree—
labors done,
questions answered,
perplexities solved—
to realize
with unfathomable joy
that I will never again
  find myself
    bewildered.

Mother Love
by Meredith Horst

I wanted a child that looked like my husband. It didn't happen. Instead, my husband says all his children have dark hair and eyes like their mother.

Even though my children do not look like my husband, I would not trade these children for any who may have been born to us. As our social worker told us when we were starting our first adoption, "My husband and I think any children who could have been born to us would have been **inferior** to the ones we adopted." At that time, I did not know the intensity of a mother's love, that fierce possession. But she's so right! These are my children! I just love their Korean faces, their skin, their black hair, their noses, their eyes.

Sometimes my children do not want to be Asian. They want to look like us, to have been born to us. Yes, I agree that I would love to have borne them. But I could not have. They could only be who they are by having been born to Korean birthparents. I would not change who they are. I love them this way. Thence, I walk the adoptive mother path of trying to empathize with their feelings while thinking, *No, don't bother to look like me. I like you this way!*

Everywhere we go everyone talks about who looks like whom and where so-and-so gets that and who the new baby looks like. At such times I wonder what my children are thinking. Sometimes we need to get with other adoptive families so our children know we are not alone.

At an adoption meeting my daughter points. "That little girl looks like me!"

"Sure enough," I smile back. That little girl's mother and I discuss how our children like to see other children who look like them.

That mother looks at us and says, "But sure you look alike. Of course you do. You both have dark hair and eyes." My daughter and I smile at each other. Of course! We are mother and daughter. No matter what others see, we belong together! Love, not looks, makes me a mother.

Unborn Love
by Becky Newswanger

It was not ours—
the life we had embraced;
But yet within our hearts
this soul was placed.
And though we knew
we really had no claim,
We loved our little one
who had no name.
Today the tender hope
we felt is gone;
Our eagerness increased
for heaven's dawn.

Little Blue Shoe—Lost!
by Tina Fehr

They were small and cute and bright blue—and they were half price! My little son saw them, too, and instantly it was as though they were his. Seeing his delight, I made the purchase.

For Joshua these little blue shoes were synonymous to romping outdoors. Each morning after breakfast, he brought them to me. "Ou'side?" he lisped.

Then after one evening out, one of the little blue shoes was missing. Had we dropped it at the park? But I was sure I'd seen them both on his feet as we came indoors.

So we searched the house. We trailed all the places Joshua likes to visit. The toy box, the toothbrush drawer, the cereal cupboard. No little blue shoe.

Perhaps we left it at someone's house. "Grandma, did you see Joshua's shoe?" No, she hadn't. The aunties were queried. No little blue shoe.

Maybe one of us had scooped it up with things we were putting away. Each drawer was searched, each piece of furniture inspected, the storage closet plundered. No little blue shoe.

Then several weeks later . . .

"Joshua's shoe!" my oldest son pranced into the kitchen holding the errant footwear above his head.

"The little blue shoe is found!" I exclaimed. I retrieved the lonely left shoe and put both on Joshua's feet. He beamed and toddled toward the front door. "Ou'side?"

I called my husband at work. "Rejoice with us. The little blue shoe is found!"

Grandmother and the aunties must be told too. "Rejoice with us. The little blue shoe is found!"

My thoughts drifted to long ago. There had been one lost sheep, one lost coin, one lost sinner. And when each was found, joy radiated from the hearts of the seeker, inviting others to share in the gladness.

Luke 15:10 tells of a heavenly company that expresses joy when a lost soul is found—angels! "Likewise, I say unto you, there is joy in the presence of the angels of God over one sinner that repenteth."

I begin asking myself questions . . .

When a brother or sister in the church confesses sin, do I hold a grudge . . . or do I rejoice?

When someone apologizes for being unkind, do I pout . . . or do I rejoice?

When God shows me my sins and failures, do I despair . . . or do I repent and then rejoice?

I hear angels calling me to join in the celebration over that which was lost and now is found . . . whether a lost little blue shoe or a penitent soul released to freedom!

Her Job in the Kingdom of God
by Tina Fehr

She draws strength from God's living water
and she glorifies God.
She takes many moments to pray
and she glorifies God.
She cooks and bakes and presents on tables for dozens
and she glorifies God.
She opens her mouth to bring forth songs and kind words
and she glorifies God.
She flies across ocean waters or crosses a street corner
to tell about Jesus
and she glorifies God.
She washes and scrubs and the clothes come out crisp and clean
and she glorifies God.
She teaches with patience, love, and kindness
and she glorifies God.
She creates and makes and gives a gift
and she glorifies God.
She places a flower here and a sprig there
and the occasion is delightful to the eyes
and she glorifies God.
She helps her darling husband
and she glorifies God.
She takes a small hand in hers
and she glorifies God.

She knows just what to buy and where and when
and she glorifies God.
She cuts and arranges in jars and in winter they eat the fruits thereof
and she glorifies God.
She rubs with a cloth and swishes with long handles
and the places gleam
and she glorifies God.
She digs a small hole and puts in something smaller yet;
She waters it and watches it grow
and she glorifies God.
She cuddles and rocks and guides little ones
and she glorifies God.
She sheds a tear for some soul
and she glorifies God.
She takes fabric, cuts it into various pieces,
and sews it into one piece again
and she glorifies God.
She wears a smile and the beautiful garment of praise
and she glorifies God.
She makes big ideas little for young minds
and she glorifies God.
She bandages wounds and encourages the brokenhearted
and she glorifies God.

---

*"Let your light so shine before men,
that they may see your good works, and glorify your
Father which is in heaven."*
MATTHEW 5:16

*"I will praise thee, O Lord my God, with all my heart:
and I will glorify thy name for evermore."*
PSALM 86:12

All the Way to the "Son"
by Loura D. Nolt

"Mommy, I love you all the way to the sun!" The sweet voice of my six-year-old daughter floated to my ears as I sat trying to write a letter. I smiled at her and rewarded her with a big happy hug.

"I love you all the way to the moon!" I replied. It is a game all my children play with us. To see who can say they love the most.

As she skipped away again, pigtails bouncing, instantly my mind went to earlier that same week. I thought of how frustrated I had gotten at that same little girl. How I despaired that day at her unwillingness to help and be cheerful.

I am just so thankful that my children forgive me and still love me even when I so often stumble and do them wrong. Their forgiveness comes so quickly. Their love is so complete.

I recalled the day when I needed to deal out a punishment to my four-year-old son. Moments later with tears still glistening on his tender cheeks, he came bounding through the door with a handful of those glorious yellow dandelions that attract little ones like bees. "Flowers for you, Mommy!" he chirped, having completely moved on from the session. Love and forgiveness flowing from his dear little heart.

Lord, help me be like them, I prayed. Immediately, through my mind, floated a picture of someone. I knew exactly why and what God was saying. A shiver went up my spine. He may as well have said these words out loud.

"You need to forgive."

Why couldn't I be like these "little ones?" Why did I struggle so much to forgive someone whom I felt had wronged us?

My mind wandered over the situation we are currently facing due to what I considered "injustices" against us and others. I thought I had forgiven. I told myself it wasn't really my problem. They are the ones that did it. Therefore, I allowed myself to think that a few irritable thoughts were justifiable in this particular situation.

But I am <u>wrong</u>. There is no room for unforgiveness in the life of those who follow Christ. "Forgive us our debts as we forgive our debtors (those who trespass against us)." The only reason I felt trespassed against was because I didn't forgive, didn't move on, didn't ask for God's help to see the situation clearly. I kept our opinion at the forefront and didn't want to see theirs.

My thoughts went again to my children as it does so many times. (I think God allowed for me to become a mother because He knew they would teach me so much!)

Those pure innocent little ones could so often hold grudges against us as parents. There are many times when I judge a situation before I hear clearly what is going on. Many times when I grow frustrated and speak unkindly or become rushed and trod without thought over their feelings.

Yes, we mothers would surely be up against if we didn't receive forgiveness from our offspring.

A bunch of weedy broken flowers. An "I love you all the way to the sun!" Whatever it takes to remind me of my areas of weaknesses. Then I can clearly pray, Lord, help me be like them in forgiveness as well.

By forgiving, I can love those that hurt me, "All the way to the Son!"

A Safe Shelter
by Faith Sommers

OUR HOME—a shelter
    from the elements; cozy in winter, shaded in summer.
    from outside influences; unhealthy peer pressure,
        unwholesome friendships.
Where we can flourish as God made us,
    Where we can grow toward Him,
        spread our wings and learn to fly;
    rising, falling—no one laughs, all encourage.
Where someone misses us when we're gone,
    always welcomes us,
        always supports,
            and always loves.
From a million stresses . . .
    Our home is a safe shelter.

THE CHURCH—a shelter
    from the world; its sinful allurements, its fears, hurts, loneliness, its downward spiral.
    from ourselves; our pride (she calls us to humility), our aloofness (she calls us to fellowship), our critical eye (she shows us the path of love).
    from the enemy; his desire to have our souls is thwarted by our love for God and our stability in a Scriptural church.
    By the prayers of the saints, by our commitment to God Who is the greatest of all, and Who has promised that the gates

of hell cannot prevail against this safe harbor:
    the church.
The safest shelter: my Lord and my God.
    When I'm lonely, when I'm fearful, when I'm rejoicing, when I'm victorious
        God has been my safe shelter, my strong tower.
            Unto Him will I run
                when I need a friend Who always understands . . .
                when life is too much, and my strength is too small.

        Thank you, God,
    for the shelters You have provided for me.

On Bringing Up Difficult Children
by Darletta F. Martin

Some ladies raise petunia beds
With pink and purple flowers
That dance among the whites and reds
And seldom tax their powers.
The beauty of their weedless sway
My thorny bed exposes.
I daily water, prune, and pray
    That it may
        bring forth
            roses.

Moving Along With Reality
by Anita Martin

I WAS A GIRL...

I lay on my back in the apple orchard and watched the fluffy clouds in all their intriguing, endless action . . . floating on and on, changing shape and then finally melting away. I had many things to think about and somehow the great span of the sky helped me to understand my heart and mind. I saw God in the endless blue . . . I felt His greatness, His infinity, His power. I sank into the blueness and thought about heaven, mansions of gold, and no tears. I "flew" with the birds and pondered God's promises that say He will give us wings as eagles . . . how free! How breathtaking! I thought of our spirits and how they meet with God's Spirit as He teaches us about His tender love for each one of his children . . . His plan and purpose for each one of our lives. There was nothing as close to heaven as looking up into the face of the endless sky where earthly troubles sailed away on the tail-end of a fluffy cloud; where dreams always came true, and the harshness of reality faded into perfect bliss.

I AM A MOTHER...

I miss the time on my back in the grass, having a touch with the Creator of the earth and evading the harshness everyday living can bring with it. Mothering can seem like a rough interruption, especially if I am trying to "enjoy the clouds." The realities of motherhood have no respect for a mom that is "on her back in the grass" . . . soon there are four children piled on top of her with all the noise and laughter combined. It gives me the urge to cover my ears and close my eyes, or maybe to tell them to leave at once. I am tempted to long for the white clouds in the endless blue where troubles simply dissolve . . . on earth they bubble up around me, threatening to choke out the joy of living. But I realize I am busy creating a home where Dad and Mom need to be at home with a light of welcome on in the window; a place where new little faces and hearts come to join us, a place of togetherness, a place of love, and a family circle. I am busy creating something that will go on for eternity, something we hope will bring much glory and honor to the Creator of the Sky . . . souls that will be willing to be loved by Him and used by Him. I need to teach my little ones to work in a faithful way each day, helping them to face and enjoy real life with all its joys and sorrows . . . simply because dreaming children and moms on their backs won't accomplish much for anyone, including themselves.

I MIGHT BE A GRANDMA . . .

If I ever am a grandma, maybe I will have time to lie on my back in the grass again and enjoy the tickly grass and fluffy clouds . . . think about God and dream about heaven. But I think I will have learned something about combining reality with it.

CHATTERBOX
by Darla Weaver

My little boy is beside me, talking in his sweet baby voice. He is always beside me, this little one who will soon be three years old, and he's always talking.

His subjects are as varied as the colors and shapes of a kaleidoscope, his pronunciations funny and dear, his accents charming. It makes me look at the world with new eyes when I hear his version of it translated into toddler language. The daily things become enthralling and the mundane exciting. His observations brighten many hours with laughter and smiles.

And he's so lovable. Nor is he afraid to voice it. "Daddy, I love you so much," he says, wrapping his arms around Daddy's neck. "Mom, I just love you," he says, and I get a hug. It reminds me to also be open and generous with my love for my family. Today, not next week or next year.

We love this little chatterbox who brightens our lives. We also love this talkative stage. But sometimes I forget what a treasure these hours hold. When he's been attached to my side for hours, talking non-stop while I'm doing my version of multi-tasking, I begin to feel smothered—overwhelmed by words, dozens and dozens of words.

I overheard him and his older sister at play yesterday. "I do wish you wouldn't ask so many questions," she finally exclaimed in exasperated tones. And promptly on the heels of the impatient words, she added, "But I guess it's not very nice of me to say that."

Then I think of mothers I know, dealing with the opposite difficulty, teenagers who will not talk, though they could. Older children and troubled ones, those who decline all help, building walls of silence instead of bridges with words. I wonder if someday this precocious toddler, who now won't stop talking, will seal his lips to me and refuse to start.

I hope not. But thinking about it helps me to remember to cherish this time. He won't be three forever, this talkative toddler who's always underfoot. I remember to love this stage too, for what it is—the stage of questions without number and words that won't stop. The chatterbox stage.

BARBER MEDITATIONS
by Lydia Hess

It only takes a minute for Daddy to employ
The shears and - Gulp! - change baby into a little boy.
Though locks fall in an instant to decorate the floor,
It takes a mound of moments and many lessons more
To change the youthful laddie into a full-grown man . . .
I whisper to the Father, "Alone I never can
Convert my son to manhood. Take out the snippers; then
Lop off the wayward curls. Make him a man.
Amen."

"Can I Laugh Ya?"
by Sheila Petre

My two-year-old daughter was playing in the living room with me. She would climb up beside the couch and nose-dive over the arm of it. "Mommy, watch!" she hollered. "I'm gonna make you laugh. I'm gonna make you laugh." She dove over the edge and emerged giggling. "Mommy, did I laugh ya? Mommy can I laugh ya again?"

I was trying to balance the household budget at the time, and didn't have a whole lot of room for humor left at the end of the month. But Rachael's repeated efforts finally drew a grin. Her giggle is contagious.

Since, I think of her question almost daily. "Can I laugh ya?" We all need to be "laughed" occasionally these days. Whether we are trying to choose between milk or eggs as the item we could more easily cut back on in our grocery spending; whether we are worried about our friend's cancer . . . or how we will cope in the future if Jesus doesn't return as soon as we are beginning to believe He will . . . we need a little laughter. Laughter releases the pressures that build up within us—and does us good like medicine. The Scriptures have been telling us this all our lives.

So where can we look for humor?

Even in the Scriptures. I found an unexpectedly funny verse in the King James Version of the Bible the other day. I can't believe it was there all along and I never noticed it. Look up Job 21, verse 3. Job speaking. "Suffer me that I may speak, and after that I have spoken, mock on." The evening I read this, I laughed and read it aloud: "After that I have spoken, mock on." Have you ever felt this way? This isn't the first time Job's tortured tongue let loose a laughable line of satire. He says a similar thing about his friends several pages before this, in verse 2 of chapter 12: "No doubt but ye are the people, and wisdom shall die with you."

This quote pops up in my mind with a quirky little grin every time I begin to think that my own opinion far surpasses, for wisdom, the opinions of those around me. "No doubt," my mind mocks on, "but ye are the people and wisdom shall die with you."

And I have proof of my own fallibility. I myself am an astonishing source of humor sometimes. Laughing at one's self is some of the best medicine around. Have you ever done it? Rachael locked me in our attic one day. It wasn't her fault. I should have been more careful to prop the door open when I went upstairs. Rachael simply shut the door behind me. Our attic has no inside latch. My tears were postponed by an acute sense of the incongruity of me racing around the attic barefoot and with my hair undone, screaming for help. I scolded my daughter from behind the door. I hollered. I choked back a tear or two with a little giggle. I prayed. I pounded on the cobwebby attic windows, even though not a soul was in sight. My mother-in-law, who lives just down the hill, and was outside, finally rescued me. She said she had heard a strange sound and thought maybe it was an ailing engine in a passing car.

Well. Thanks for the compliment on my lovely voice.

I've told the attic story to various friends since, and it always brings a smile or laugh. Laughter pockets fill the skirts of every common day. Have you found some lately? Feel free to pass them on. We always feel better when someone "laughs" us.

Is Your House Clean?
by Anita Martin

What really does God want of me and my housekeeping? Let's say I'm a model lady . . . I keep my house perfectly clean and everyone admires and becomes jealous by turns. Whenever anyone drops in, they testify to its spotless condition . . . all the other homes they visited were battling piles of wash and muddy floors. I was found sitting at the sewing machine with my kitchen in picture album shape.

What would you think if you knew my family had to patiently endure a very controlling mom/wife day after day as I pursued my goals? What would you think if you saw how abrupt I was with my neighbor lady or how much I scolded my child for the tracks he left on the shining floor? What would you think if you saw the drive to do everything a certain way so that everything holds out in a predictable fashion? Unpredictable things were earthshaking and thus not allowed!! What would you think if you knew I spent hours cleaning and organizing things when I should have been rocking the children and reading to them? What would you think if you saw me unwilling to make a meal for the visitors in the area because it would "mess up my kitchen?" I think you would see it. I think you would know that *perfection* has become my idol.

We ask why this is wrong . . . doesn't God require us to reach up to the high standard of perfection in our work and also in our spiritual lives? We want to be *outstanding* Christians . . . ones that are filled with Bible teaching and blessed with a godly and golden heritage. We dutifully fulfill all we think a truly seasoned Christian does, which ends up putting out an astounding display of perfection that both intimidates and deceives others. As things become more and more mechanical, unreal, and controlling, we become blinded to the way pride and hardness of heart twists itself all around our way of relating to life and the people in it.

How about being real about things? Is perfection a *true* picture of how things are? Are you ashamed to admit you are flawed, imperfect, needy, and struggling? When we put an emphasis on perfection we make others uncomfortable, stiff, and fearful because in reality our world is just the opposite. While they stand back and admire it, they do not feel at home in the presence of perfection because they don't fit . . . and they never will as long as they see their own neediness before God. We are the ones who are smug about our predictable and sensible procedures on how to attain this wonderful state. We are the ones blinded to the actual state of things, unaware that things in reality are rotting, filthy, and falling apart.

Living for God is so different. We keep our houses orderly but allow the scenes to change according to what the day brings. We allow people to be human, make mistakes, and help them with the "give and take" of life. We relax the reigns of control and stop trying to protect our lovely image of perfection. We don't live in denial of what we are really like . . . we can actually relax and be normal, faltering humans that allow God to do things as He wants. As a result, we feel with and become involved in the lives of others.

God wants to use us as we are . . . He brings honor to Himself through our weakness. He needs humble, serviceable, creative, welcoming, orderly, and very useful houses—homes. After all, we don't want to be *perfectly useless,* do we?

ON CALL
by Darla Weaver

I was stealing a few moments of solitude, seated as I was in another room, reading a page or two of my present book. Briefly I drifted blissfully away . . .

But peace only lingered for a minute or less. In the adjoining room I heard those toddling footsteps with their uneven pattering becoming firmer. More urgent. He was a baby on a mission now, and that mission was to find Mom. The moment he realizes that I am out of sight he goes from relaxed to resolute.

Jabbering baby language in a rather resentful voice, he trots into the room where I am hiding in plain sight. Then it is like sunshine and blue skies breaking through where just before gray clouds had hovered from horizon to horizon.

Baby eyes light up. Baby grins extinguish the frowns, and happy chatter replaces the scolding gibberish. He runs toward me.

"Here I am," I laugh resignedly. "Run to earth again." I lay aside my book and pick up my baby to cuddle.

Our other two children were already school-aged when Matthan arrived to bless our lives with such charm and joy. We learned anew just how much love and laughter one small life contains. Also, we learned again of the time, frustration, and tears that are invested in the life of a child, not to mention the dollars, the worries, the sleepless nights, and the equally napless days.

To be sure, I loved that bit of humanity that we wrapped into cozy pastel blankets, that we cuddled and bathed and lotioned, rocked and fed and changed. It was such fun to care for a little one again.

But I had also loved my peaceful days. Call me strange and unusual, but I had liked the stage of life at which I thought I had arrived. I sent my children off to school each morning and then started the day as I had planned it. My weeks were filled with all the duties of homemaking—planned ahead, charted, mapped out—each task fitting into its allotted hours without much fuss. I enjoyed the pleasant rhythm of my days, especially the hours I had to myself each day for the pursuit of my own dreams. I liked the serene existence I had most of the time.

Enter baby dear. When Matthan was born my peaceful patterns of living, my scheduled environment, and my hours of solitude all drifted out every available door and window. I was on call again, and needed to learn the discipline required to put a baby's needs before my own wants.

It wasn't such a big task, considering how much I loved the dear little thing who needed me now, every hour of every day. I was happy to care for his needs, and his life blessed my own in ways I couldn't have imagined.

But sometimes . . . sometimes I really wanted to be alone again for a little while. That's why I had sneaked to a cushioned chair in another room and sat down to read a few pages in my book.

But Matthan, who is now a toddler, doesn't seem to share my desire for a bit of solitude. On the contrary, he delights in being constantly by my side. So when he grins gleefully at having found my hiding place, I smile in return and lay aside my book.

After all, I have learned that by the time I've changed the calendars a few more times, he will be off to school too. He won't even care anymore that I'm not beside him every single minute of every single day.

As I caress his silky baby hair, I think about his dependence on me. It resembles my own dependence on God. Like Matthan wants me close by to respond to his every need, so I wish for God to stay by my side as I enter each new day. In fact, I expect God to be on call for me.

Matthan is content when he knows I'm nearby. He thrives in my loving care. Although I don't give in to each whim and demand in his life, he knows I haven't ever neglected to care for him.

In the same way I thrive in God's constant care. He has promised never to leave me. Even when He doesn't give me each desire of my heart, satisfy every whim I have and every demand I make, I know He's caring for me.

I rest in Him, knowing that "Before they call I will answer; and while they are yet speaking I will hear." (Isaiah 65:24)

He's always there, and He's always listening. He hasn't closed the doors of heaven to enjoy a few seconds of silence without the constant demands of humanity. He's always on call for me.

Humbling Realization
by Lydia Hess

My youngsters often watch as I
Roll out another crust for pie;
They want to help. But do I dare
Leave flaky shells within their care?

I'm humbled when I pause and see
The tender youth about my knee—
The souls that God entrusts to me.

This Is Not That Bad
by Sylvia Yoder

I am nearing middle age. Gone are the preconceived ideas and notions of my teens and early twenties. Long gone. Today I stand where I dreaded; middle aged, long past newly-wed, and now a mother of school children.

It used to look boring; how naive I was. Is a mother of active, mischievous toddlers and school girls full of stories ever bored? Busy, yes! Bored? Never!

I didn't know back then how it felt to victoriously turn from scrubbing a sink full of dresses now swishing in the washer, to behold two busy little children, two boxes of cereal, and a container of dried beans all mixed together on the kitchen floor.

I feel flat, tired, like laughing and crying all mixed together. But not bored. And I realize this is not that bad.

Back when I was serving at every wedding and found occasions in between for new dresses, it sounded awful to hear the moms tell of their destitute supply of dresses. They were busy sewing for growing girls.

Today that's me; plus I've cut up some of my scarce, ill-fitting supply to make dresses for my girls. Do I feel destitute? No, my arms are full even if my closet is empty. My husband loves me, new dresses or not. Besides, when two beaming, bouncing girls in matching dresses head out the door for school, I feel rich. Yes, maybe a little shabby but not destitute. And I realize this is not that bad.

The tales they told about their children washing dishes have become reality at my house. It sounded so distressing! Was it really worth all the mess?

I still wonder when I'm doing dishes with a toddler on a stool on both sides of me. Until my eight year old pushes her stool up to the sink and says, "I'll wash the dishes, Mama." The drainer is topsy-turvy, but the dishes are relatively clean. And I realize this is not that bad.

To everything there is a time and a season. I want to enjoy the good and make the best of the not-so-good in this season. For school girls grow into teenagers, and teenagers don't throw their arms around your waist stoutly declaring, "You are the best Mama in the world!" Teenagers don't run back into the house for a good-bye kiss before they head out for the day.

And what adds more spice than toddlers? The sleep lost in these years is toothaches and tummy aches, not heartaches. Ahhh, teenagers . . . maybe, just maybe, when I get there I'll realize, this is not that bad.

To everything there is a season,
and a time for every stage of motherhood:
A time to give birth, and a time to enjoy the end
of child-bearing years.
A time to plant, and a time to pull out those old,
frosted tomato vines.
A time to kill the old chickens and a time to bottle feed
the triplet goat who now resides in the bathtub.
A time to tear out the moldy bathroom floor and a time to add
on the long-awaited dining room.
A time to weep over the erring one and a time to laugh
at the sheer ingeniousness of childish imagination.
A time to mourn over the smashed puppy,
and a time to skip in the rain under an umbrella.
A time to cast stones from the freshly-tilled garden

and a time to gather stones to build a backyard stone fort.
A time to hug, and a time to use the rod of correction.
A time to get groceries, and a time to lose the diaper bag in the mall!
A time to keep old clothes for carpet rags, and a time to cast away the decrepit leftovers in the back of the fridge.
A time to tear up those carpet rag clothes, and a time to sew those school program dresses before tomorrow evening arrives!
A time to keep silent rather than speak in anger, and a time to speak a word of appreciation for a job well done.
A time to love the unlovely adolescent, and a time to hate the sin that lies at our own heart's door.
A time of war on the clutter that plagues every housewife, and a time of peace relaxing on the porch at sunset.

"What profit hath she that worketh in that wherein she laboreth? God hath made everything beautiful in HIS time."
(Ecclesiastes 3:1-9, 11 paraphrased.)

This is the secret of contentment in whatever phase of motherhood we find ourselves. In every age and stage it is the grace of God, in spite of us, not because of us, that helps us press on day after day. Let's enjoy the present. Then we can have a past with few regrets and a future brightened by the promises of God.

Why Didn't You Tell Me?
by L. D. Nolt

It was snack time. My children, ages three and two, were enjoying a snack of little cracker fish. As I "visited" with them, I mentioned the fact that tomorrow Daddy had off of work because of Ascension Day.

"What is Ascension Day, Mommy?" wondered Seth. At three he was always inquisitive and eager to learn. Many times I grew weary of the constant questions, but he wasn't deterred by a flippant answer. He always needed to know any and all details.

"It is the day we remember that Jesus ascended up into Heaven after He had been crucified on the cross," I said, but I could see there were more questions coming. I quickly went on.

"You see, after Jesus was killed by a lot of angry people who didn't understand Him, they buried Him in a big hole made out of rock." The children nodded, remembering their Bible storybook with pictures.

"He did not stay in the hole though, but in three days He rose again. Then it went forty days that He stayed on earth and after those forty days, one day He was with His friends and suddenly He rose into the air and was taken back up into Heaven."

"Why did He go back into Heaven?" he asked. "Didn't He like it down here?"

How could I explain this simply and yet thoroughly so that he could understand? "He had done all that He needed to do on earth and now it was time for Him to go up into Heaven where He is waiting for us to come someday," I explained as I replenished their supply of snack.

"And you know what is really special?" I said, "He promised that someday He will come again! Just like He went. Someday the clouds will roll back and we will see Him with our own eyes!" In my own excitement I looked out the window toward the sky.

Even my little two-year-old daughter was listening now. They both looked out the window at the clear blue sky, eyes wide with wonder. It was enough to keep me going and I went on feeling that tremor of excitement.

"Yes, the Bible says that every eye will see Him and everyone will bow down to Him. He will come and take us home to Heaven to be with Him forever! There will be no more tears or sad people; no more hurt or 'ouchies' or any bad days. We will always be together—no more going to work for Daddy or saying goodbye to anyone!"

I felt my voice choking up as I thought of the glory of an eternity with Jesus. But mixed in with that joy was also the concern that every parent has; oh that my children may all choose to walk in the truth. They were innocent and little now.

And the next words out of my son's mouth proved his sweet innocence; "Why didn't you ever tell me, Mommy?! I never knew that Jesus would come like that!"

His sweet smile was so innocent and full of wonder as He thought of all that would entail. He and his sister went on for a few minutes listing people we wouldn't have to say goodbye to like Grandmas and Grandpas, cousins, aunts, uncles and friends. They also thought maybe they wouldn't have to wear shoes! Or use the bathroom!

But my mind stayed back at his innocent yet timely phrase, "Why didn't you ever tell me, Mommy?" Now I know he is only three years old and maybe only now was able to comprehend a little of what I was saying, but my thoughts went many directions.

What about my neighbors? And friends? Would they have reason to say those very words, "Why didn't you ever tell me?" Maybe I don't need to go around pushing it at them, but have I been approachable? Have I led the kind of life that shows what I cannot always say; that I have a Savior whom I am living for? Whom I would be willing to die for? Have I shown hospitality and kindness? Am I submissive that by looking at our marriage others can see evidence of God in our lives?

I thought of that old hymn titled "You Never Mentioned Him to Me." When given the opportunity do I mention my Lord on a daily basis? Have I given Him the credit for my blessings? For any success we may have in our family, have I given glory and honor to the One to whom it belongs?

I thought ahead to that great and notable day when the Lord himself shall come. Will there be people around me that I have brushed shoulders with on a regular basis that could say the words, "Why didn't you ever tell me?!"

John 4:35 says, "Behold, I say unto you, Lift up your eyes, and look on the fields; for they are white already to harvest."

We have been truly blessed to have been raised in a way that we can have the truth of God's word at our fingertips. May we never pass up an opportunity to help with the harvest in the vineyard of the Lord!

My House and God's
by Sylvia Yoder

It is a new day. I sit in the corner of the couch, Bible on my lap, and steaming mug of coffee in my hand. The house is still except for the occasional rustle of papers in the office where my husband is doing paperwork and checking emails. The world is quiet in the predawn peace, unbroken by the rush and noise of the coming day.

I hear bare feet; the day is about to begin in earnest. My children creep from their cozy nests of slumber; one by one they join me on the couch. They drag their blankets with them, and we become a tangled heap of arms and legs and little bodies, still warm and drowsy, loath to fling aside the cloak of night in exchange for the garb of coming day.

A bottle for the baby replaces my coffee cup. My Bible lies on the end table; the last five verses of John 20 can wait until tomorrow morning. My children are awake. I must greet this day. I look at my brood, tousled heads and flushed cheeks. I smell their morning breath and a stale nighttime diaper. My four year old sucks his pacifier; I notice it squeaks with every suck. I look at him and wonder—how do I have a four year old still doing *that?* I was the mother who wasn't going to allow *that*. What have I become? How did *that* happen and I don't even care? He hides his "nip" under his pillow during the day, unless life gets too rough, and then he slips upstairs for a few comforting sucks. I am smiling. When did something I wasn't going to allow become something that makes me smile?

Motherhood! Oh, how it has changed me. Before I began motherhood I didn't know so much love could exist under a tangled heap of blankets, "snugglers" waiting for the sun to rise and thrust us into the day.

Oh no! Back then I lived a life of "attack and conquer." I set out to accomplish my goals for the day and I succeeded.

Then I met my first child. That was nine years ago. Nine years of motherhood. I look at her on the far end of the couch. Poor child, I learned so much at her expense, but she seems no worse for the wear. She is a forgiving one.

Next came number two. By this time I had learned the "divide and conquer" method, but that didn't work either. This one came into the world needy and demanding. My eyes rest on her, so much restless energy to channel. So many "I love you, mama" notes collecting in the box upstairs. I learned to survive instead of conquer, and slowly, slowly I learned to live.

"Look at the sky." A sleepy voice jolts my reverie. I look out the window and see a faint pink glow just above the horizon. We watch as it spreads into glowing orange and liquid yellow. The world is semi-dark, the trees waving shadowy branches against the brightening sky. Time stops for a moment. The day is waiting for the sun.

Across the land many mothers and children are starting the day in many different ways, but on this morning my children and I are a wonderful, tangled heap on the couch. An hour from now the older ones will be fresh and shiny, ready for another day of school. The little ones will have breakfast scrubbed from their faces and be leaping over piles of clothes as I sort laundry. But for now we snuggle and yawn (and the "nip" squeaks with every suck). We watch God paint the morning sky.

The light is brighter now and shines in the window. I study the window—the grime that collects faster than I can wash it off, fingerprints from the children who look out, pawprints from the pets who look in. Back when I lived the "attack and conquer" life, I know that window was clean. But did I see the sun come up? Or was my back to the sun as I washed that window?

Ahh! This is better, to face the rising sun. I have learned to live. The little people all crowded too close on this couch have slowed me down and taught me how to live. "If we watch closely we can see the sun when it shoots up into the sky," I tell them.

"Who powwed the sun?" demands the two year old.

"What do you mean?" I ask.

"Who powwed the sun?" she repeats, pounding my chest with her little fists.

"No one, dear; what do you mean?"

"You said, 'the sun shoots up into the sky,'" my oldest says. We laugh together at the little lass who still stares up at me with large, bewildered eyes.

And then the brilliant sun bursts forth in all its glory. We squint with eyes that water and blink, and declare with joy and wonder, "I saw the sun come up!" It beams in our window; all I see is the sunshine of a new day. Above the painted colors the sky is blue, "and above the blue is heaven, the house of God," I tell my children.

I swing my feet to the floor, sliding little bodies aside. "Time to start the day. I need girls to set the breakfast table." The morning rush is on.

Later when the school girls are out the door and semi-calm descends in my kitchen, I look down into the gray-blue eyes of my boy. "Mama," he says, "can you cut this tag off my shirt? It pokes my neck."

"Yes, my son, I can do that." I open the drawer for a pair of scissors. This drawer is like my life, always full and overflowing with stuff. It dumps stuff out the back onto the cereal boxes below when it's really full. I kneel beside my son; our eyes are level.

"Mama," he begins, and I know it's a question coming. He is

full of questions. Questions I can't answer about trucks, sale barns, and bulldozers. "Mama, when will we go to God's heaven?"

Ahh! I know this answer; I press him close. "We will go when God calls for us and only God knows when that day will be. Until then we will just live here, all together, in our little, old house." He smiles, and I am glad. Glad to live, glad that today we watched the sunrise and talked of heaven. Glad that my children can face this day with the glow of heaven in their hearts and their faces toward the sun.

I put my scissors back into the too-full drawer. My eyes linger. I savor the sight. It is earthly, fleeting, temporal. In my heavenly mansion there won't be a drawer that dumps its excess on the cereal boxes. I turn and face this day with JOY.

Psalm 113:3,4,9 "From the rising of the sun unto the going down of the same the Lord's name is to be praised. The Lord is high above all nations, and His glory above the heavens. He maketh the barren woman to keep house, and to be a joyful mother of children. Praise ye the Lord."

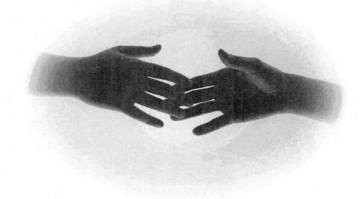

Beauty at Night
by Lucille Martin

"He's so cute in the middle of the night," I told my husband repeatedly when our son was a newborn. The difficulty of getting up several times each night to feed him was tempered by the reward of seeing his adorable little face in the semi-darkness. I loved when the dim glow of the microwave light caught a reflected sparkle in the two bright eyes looking up at me. It was our special time together—just my baby and me in the rocking chair in the darkness. With his fuzzy head tucked under my chin, I was supremely content.

The months passed. My newborn became an almost one year old who still got up more than once a night. I ceased to think of him as cute in the middle of the night because I was too busy thinking about everyone else's babies who slept all night long before this age. One night, I fought my irritation—yes, he was sick, but couldn't he let me sleep a little more?—and I realized that he was still cute at midnight. His hair isn't soft anymore; it's been cut too often for that, but I still like to rub it, and his cheek still carries a dimple. I studied him in the glow of a nightlight and marveled again at the innocence and peace on his small, sleeping face. *He's still adorable at night*, I thought. Was it possible that he hadn't changed—but I had? "I haven't slept all night for over a year," I had complained to my husband.

I miss my happy baby. He's whiny and clingy right now—a stage I don't enjoy very much. He's fighting a cold; are his teeth hurting? I wish I knew. Last night—or rather, this morning, but it still felt like night to me—he refused to settle down and go back to sleep. I lay beside him and he wiggled and twisted and squirmed. His eyes were closed, but every few minutes he cried out and tossed and turned. I let him lie on my chest, but he was still restless. He seemed to be trying to sleep, but something was obviously bothering him. I fought frustration. If only he could tell me what was wrong! All this fussing and fighting when he should be sleeping . . . and I had no idea what to do for him. Finally, after he had cried enough to wake Daddy, and after I had tried to hold him in all the positions I could think of, he calmed down and fell asleep leaning against me. I eased him into bed, and covered him with his soft pawprints blanket. And he's still asleep.

I could be frustrated because he waited to sleep good until after I had to get up. Or because I know I will be tired today because the night was too short. But when I peek into his room, I can't possibly be frustrated. He is the picture of perfect peace; mouth open, arms thrown out, totally relaxed. He is adorable.

And I thank God for him. Yes, I lose sleep for him. Yes, his wailing irritates me. But I love him. He is my son, and he is a gift from God.

When the Thought Counts

by Lucille Martin

I was a teenager the day Myron brought me a dandelion. Or rather, what had been a dandelion.

To be exact, it was the remains of a gray-haired, gone-to-seed dandelion, with all but two or three hair blown away. But I loved Myron, and when he brought me that stem, I thanked him and I meant it. And I wrote a poem which I gave to his mother.

GOLDEN GIFT
Just a long, long stem and a bit of fuzz
Where the head of a dandelion was;
But it came to me in the grubby fist
Of a little boy. Though he sadly missed
The brighter flowers he might have brought,
I saw behind it the loving thought.
No beauty of flower, no bright bouquet;
Just a gift of love on a lovely day.

Its gold is gone, but I still enjoy
The gold in the heart of a little boy.

Myron was the little boy who lived down the road, and whom we babysat sometimes. He was special because he came after a gap in his family, and he was special because we watched him grow up just as we had watched his older brothers. So when he brought me a dandelion stem, I thought he was sweet, and I enjoyed it.

Today, as I enjoyed the breeze in my backyard, my one year old gave me a dandelion. Nevermind that there were bright yellow blossoms scattered through the grass; he brought me an almost headless one, with no beauty left.

And I thought, *Little boys are still the same.* Years later, and three states away in my PA backyard, my own little boy brought me the same special gift. I love him, and so I thanked him before I gave it back. He ripped off the head, and then tore the stem in two on his sharp little teeth. Then he offered me half.

Thank you, son. I'm not into eating dandelions, but I love little boys and their first attempts at giving flowers. After all, isn't it the thought that counts? My trying-to-be-nice projects don't always turn out the best, but hopefully others can see my intentions and love me anyway.

But right now it's time to wash the yellow stains from two little hands.

The boys were down on all fours
pretending to eat the carpet.

"What are you doing?" I asked.
"We're eating grass."
"What kind of animals are you?"
"We're boy animals!"

by Brenda Petre

Welcome
by Brenda Petre

You're welcome to stop in to see me today—
I'm sewing in peace while my little boys play.
It's mid-Monday morning—there are towels on my line,
A few tiny places my floor might still shine;
My dishes aren't done, but I'll do them, I think,
When I'm making lunch and I'm close by the sink.
But now with the little ones playing so nice,
I'm finishing shirt cuffs I've worked on now twice.
I don't have a system, you'll notice for sure—
I can't finish one job without starting four;
There's never a time that I truly can say,
"I did all the work that I hoped to today!"
But we are so happy; our tummies are fed.
There are clothes in our drawer, and warm sheets on each bed;
Our house is a palace—you know what I mean?
It looks kind of lived in, but moderately clean.
So stop in to see me, although you may find
I'm hardly efficient and I'm six steps behind—
But this is our prayer that each day of the year
The sunshine of love will be felt while you're here!

God Brought Us Home
by Meredith Horst

It is 5:00 a.m. in Seoul, South Korea. I drag my sleep-starved body out of bed and flop to the floor to pray. Gratitude and praise for God's tremendous blessing in giving us another son by adoption tangles with the reality that this is the day that we take him and our two year old back home to Kentucky. My prayer consists of groans of exhaustion and pleas for God to help me through the next 24-plus hours until we get to our house. I pray, "Lord, You are going to have to do it because there is no way I can."

This was Saturday morning in Korea. A long time ago it had been Sunday evening in Kentucky. We had decided to stay home from church and go to bed really early to prepare for getting up at 3:00 AM to leave on this adoption trip. We could not sleep. As the hours blinked by, my frustration mounted. This was our second adoption trip to Korea, so I knew what was ahead. I knew how tired I would be till I was home again. Yet here I was not sleeping! I did not feel rested in the least when 3:00 arrived. Over 30 hours later we were in a hotel in Seoul. It was 11:00 p.m. and I was even more exhausted than I had feared. But could I sleep much? No. My body said it was the middle of the morning.

So the rest of the week went by as we tried to fit ourselves and our two year old into the time change while dealing with the overwhelming excitement of getting our new baby. Now here we were. We had our baby in our arms! But we had to get back home.

New babies are unpredictable. Especially so when they are already eight months old, do not understand a word we say nor a song we sing, and would rather not have this strange white mother with a long nose.

God is so good. He took over and got us home in spite of my humanity. He made this new son deal with stress by just going to sleep. He gave me two kind Asian women to sit between when I could not sit beside my husband on that long flight over the Pacific Ocean. He made our two year old go to sleep for a good portion of that flight. He took away the feeling of my world spinning and jumping that comes over me when I am way beyond tired. God brought us home.

But no one can say I was not through labor.

One morning our four-year-old daughter and two-year-old son were having trouble relating. Finally I told her to play something else and let him have some peace. Immediately he begged, "I wanna piece!"

by Brenda Petre

A Reminder to Worship
by Betty Friesen

Sometimes we need the reminders of our children to open our eyes. One such time for me was on a certain Sunday morning. I was sitting in the house of God with a five month old on my lap and a daughter of three at my side.

Regretfully, I wasn't in the best spirit of worship. The July heat was creeping into the building, and for all the excuses or not I might have to be drowsy, the fact was my eyelids were drooping. Then from my side in all innocence came a blunt admonition. Three-year-old lips whispered, "We're not even praying." I opened my eyes and smiled down at her.

Another reminder came from the five month old after he had turned six already. It was a day in May when the violets were blooming, and my sister-in-law and I were hovering over them with a flower guide, trying to decide what the proper name would be for this purple spring dainty. "Common violet" was probably what it was called. Another one of those "common things," like common crow or common grackle. "It's like common worship," my son piped up. (Meaning "Come and worship/ worship Christ the newborn King.")

Common worship. How common is it for me? As common as seeing crows, grackles, and violets?

From Faith to Sight
by Betty Friesen

"That puts your due date to August 24," the doctor said briskly, squinting at the number wheel in her hand. So that was the goal of the journey we found ourselves on. This being February 28, that goal seemed like the hazy mountain peaks in the distance.

People everywhere said time was flying. For me, a most blessed woman with her seventh offspring on board, this blessed journey unwound itself slowly, one day at a time, especially in the heat of summer, teaching me patience in the meantime. And not just patience, but also perseverance. I climbed the cellar steps, pausing at the fourth step from the top, panting, wondering how my sister carrying her tenth climbed the stairs to their sleeping quarters upstairs. I tried to count my blessings at how handy it was to be carrying my littlest with me, while every so often leaning on my hoe to catch my breath.

On top of patience and perseverance it took faith. After "seeing" the baby on the computer screen during my ultrasound, so many weeks had passed that the "real" feeling had disappeared. Even as I washed and folded baby blankets and sleepers, faith barely took me beyond. Thoughts of this present clumsiness and dread of labor overtook me even while little heels kicked and churned.

"Will I really be able to love another baby?" I asked my husband.

"Oh, I think you will." My husband's faith and confidence overrode my own.

Then one wonderful day (or night) I crossed the threshhold of faith into sight. Into the realm of hearing, the reality of caressing touch. As the days went by, all the persevering effort and breathlessness proved to have been worth it, as I nuzzled his soft cheek against mine and wrapped my arms around his warm sleeping form. Gazing into his sweet, tiny face, I realized with grateful relief that for his first breath I would never again need to walk that same stretch behind me again.

While I enjoyed my present reaping, I remembered that on our journey to heaven, faith will also some wonderful day be turned into sight. We will cross the threshhold of faith into the realm of hearing angelic choruses, the reality of beholding our beloved Bridegroom. Walking the streets of gold, we will realize that the unspeakable rapture and bliss there are worth all the heat (fiery trials), all the weariness and all the panting we face on this cumbersome earth. Best of all, never again will we need to travel the miles behind us again!

SENSATION
by Lydia Hess

Our toddler thrusts a weed bouquet
Into my hands. A crude array
Of dandelion, thistle, dock,
Henbit, Queen Anne's Lace, clover mock
My floral dream of roses. Yet
I grab a vase with no regret;
I sniff the scent of servanthood,
And call the weed arrangement good.

My Loaves and Fishes
by Emeline Lehman

With a relieved sigh, I curl into the corner of the couch with my freshly-bathed baby. I have 40 minutes to feed him and comb my girls' hair before prayer meeting. *I think we're going to make it!* Jalyn is seven weeks old, but I still feel tense about getting our four children ready to go places on time. Tonight, thankfully, Levern came home in time to dress Carlos. Now we can talk while he eats supper and I feed the baby.

Levern gives me a rundown of his day spent delivering dairy supplies to farmers. *His day sounds a lot more productive than mine. Let's see . . . I fed the baby, changed the baby, saw my girls off to school, answered a thousand questions from Carlos, supervised Kelsey in making muffins after she got home from school, and . . .*

Suddenly I remember. "Oh, guess what! Yesterday I cleaned the fish aquarium and the ceiling fans in the kitchen and dining room. And today I washed some windows."

"Good for you!" My husband is used to a wife who changes the subject without notice.

"I thought I would tell you since you might not notice, and I wanted you to know I got something done besides taking care of Jalyn."

"Did you clean the ceiling fan in our bedroom? I noticed it is getting really dusty."

Bother! Why didn't I clean the one dirty fan that he had actually noticed? "Well," I say, "these fans were even dirtier. When I wiped the blades, the dirt rolled up in front of my rag and fell off in little balls onto the floor."

"Real dust bunnies, huh?"

"Yeah."

While I comb Kelsey's hair, she works on her number fact paper. She is only a few weeks into third grade, and apparently some of her number facts have evaporated during the sunny, windy summer. I should be doing flash cards with her every day, but it hasn't been happening. Heather tells me first grade stories while I comb her hair. "The second graders needed to use the word 'sad' in a sentence, and do you know what Jeffrey said? He said, 'I'm sad because my mother has cancer.'"

"Yes, it is sad," I agree. I feel guilty about how little I've been hearing school stories. Yes, I send them off with a "Have a good day," and I welcome them home with "How was school today?" but I'm so focused on my work and my grumpy baby that I haven't been really *hearing* what they say.

On our way to church, I remember that tonight is the night for "reorganization," or electing new people to fill the roles of Sunday School teachers, song leaders, and so forth. I spend most of the evening in the nursery, so it is across the nursery speaker that I hear Levern announced as the new Youth class teacher. *I wonder how that will go,* I think. *That means I get to take care of a grumpy baby and a two year old who needs a firm hand.*

The fact that I am tired makes the thought more overwhelming. While we head home, eat muffins for an after church snack, and tuck the three oldest children in bed the overwhelmed feeling grows. I reach for my Bible with more desperation than anticipation. Jalyn often insists on late night parties with activities such as fussing, eating, fussing, burping, fussing, and getting his diaper changed. Late nights and tired mornings have been taking a toll on my devotional life. I read from Luke 9 now, the story of Jesus feeding the 5,000. A familiar story, but tonight a fresh thought inspires me. The disciples faced a crowd of 5,000 men when Jesus said, "You need to give them something to eat." They must have felt a little impatient with Jesus as they replied in consternation, "How can we? We have nothing except five loaves and two fishes." But they obeyed Jesus' command to sit the people down, they waited while He thanked God for the pitifully small loaves and fishes, and then they took the bread and fish from His hands and gave them to the people to eat. The people ate, not just a nibble, but they ate and *were filled.* Another miracle.

As I look at my life, I feel a kinship to the disciples as they faced that multitude with nothing in their hands but five loaves and two fishes. My mothering responsibilities loom as overwhelming as feeding 5,000. My four children are young and innocent, but they have eternal souls. Yes, I can blame my overwhelmed feeling on weariness and hormones, but the fact remains that I am my children's mother. To pit my tired body and mind against training them as the Bible directs, seems as ridiculous as feeding the 5,000 with a bit of bread and fish.

I am forgetting the most important part of the story. *My loaves and fishes must be given to Jesus.* He can bless my pitiful store of strength and courage and multiply it to fill the needs of each day.

Thank you, Lord.

Why Do I Want to Be Well?
by Emeline Lehman

I live with depression. And anxiety. Sometimes I arrogantly hope I have left these companions in the past and they won't complicate my future, sometimes I sense them hovering like grim specters, and sometimes I feel them touch my life in physical ways.

I have gone to a doctor, laid out my symptoms, and taken the prescribed pills. I, with my husband, have spent many hours in prayer and meditation—sometimes alone, and sometimes with another trusted Christian. Taking my thoughts, feelings, pain, and fears to the Word of God, we applied the Bible to depression.

These things have helped. My depression and anxiety are controlled. I am reasonably fuctional. Someone could probably meet me and learn to know me a bit without guessing that I live with varying degrees of anxiety and depression.

But I long to be whole. To be really well. To walk without the limp.

The last few nights I have not been able to sleep well. I have had trouble falling asleep, and when I do, my sleep is riddled with troubling dreams. Yesterday, I tried taking a nap. I think I slept a little. When I was trying to get my family ready for revival meetings, though, I felt so exhausted I wondered if I could lift my arms high enough to comb my daughters' hair. We went to church and I began to feel better. After we came home and tucked the children in, I tried to read my Bible and pray. Exhaustion claimed me again, and I was thankful to snuggle into bed. I closed my eyes and waited for sleep but it was all for naught. I felt perfectly wide awake; I couldn't even imagine how it felt to be tired. *You are tired,* I told myself. *You will go to sleep.* I did. After a long time. Again to dream wildly instead of sleeping soundly.

I woke this morning feeling on the edge of an emotional disaster. *I don't think I'm going to last much longer like this,* I thought. *Better go to town, get supplies for lasagna, and get it made for the fellowship dinner on Sunday. Then if I collapse, at least that will be done.*

First, I stopped at Dorcas' to pick up a zipper that I needed to finish a sewing project. I was starting to feel desperate to feel better, somehow, some way. Sewing usually helps. I can do it almost mindlessly, and it gives me a sense of fulfillment and well-being.

I found Norma already at Dorcas' house, and Elli showed up presently. This was starting to look like a gathering of church ladies. They had coffee and I declined. I don't like coffee. I watched them, listening to them talk. I wondered about them. *Do they ever feel as I do now? What would they think if I said, "Hey, please, will you pray for me? I feel terrible."? What would happen if I plopped that down in the middle of the admiring circle around next year's planner. I wonder what they think of me. We moved into this church community nearly half a year ago. While these friends have proved dear, they have not walked with me through my darkest valleys of depression. I don't want them to. For my sake, and maybe for theirs, also.*

I left after a bit, thinking about how I obsess over wanting people to like me and worrying that they don't. My lifetime focus of desiring approval has attempted to go into overdrive since we moved. I pray about it often, desiring God's stamp of approval on my life, repeatedly shifting my focus to sharing love with others instead of desiring people's approval.

I went to Walmart, came home, finished sewing a dress, took care of my children, and the "I'm-on-the-edge-of-disaster" feeling drained away, leaving its residue of tight, knotted neck and shoulders.

We went to church again, and I came home pondering this: I wish I could be well. In fact, I wish I would never need an antidepressant. I wish I could sleep well, most of the time, without the assistance of medication. I wish I never felt uptight for unknown reasons. Feeling worried and anxious when I have a *reason* for it is normal, but when I have no reason for a feeling of impending doom—and it lurks anyway—I feel discouraged.

These wishes, oh, I have had them for months—years, in fact.

I got ready for bed, and this question came to me. I believe it came from the Holy Spirit.

Why do I want to be well?

I want my new friends to think well of me. I do not want them to ever know me as depressed, dysfunctional, dripping neediness.

Oops. I knew right away, that was a bad reason for wanting to be well. I repented of it.

This is an important question. How much do I want to be well simply because it would be more comfortable for me? My life would be easier.

That would be a notably selfish reason for wanting good health. I do acknowledge a God-given desire for good health, but is it too important in my life?

I reviewed the one thing I do know: I was created to love and glorify God.

What if depression helps me glorify God? I don't like to think of that. It's possible, and I want to be willing to suffer for His sake, but oh, I wouldn't choose depression!

I return to the original question. *Why do I want to be well?* After repenting of my desire to be well thought of and have an easier life, I went on.

When I searched my heart, laying aside the superfluous, I found only this: *I want to be a good wife and mother.*

Oh, my children! My heart bleeds for them!

I have heard tales of unhappy homes, followed by this comment, "Well, the mother (or father) had emotional struggles." Oh, how often I pray for my children, ceasing not to intercede for their souls, and petitioning God that they would not carry scars from my struggles with depression!

Oh, God! Are You there? Do You care?

Oh, God, I repent of my selfish reasons for wanting to be well. But I cling tighter to my strongest desire—to be the wife and mom that my husband and children need. And, oh God, it doesn't look possible to carry this cross and be what my family needs, but I trust You. You love them . . . and me.

I paused. A thought nudged its way to the surface, and I acknowledged it reluctantly. *What if God is using my depression to bless our family in ways I don't understand? Our God is a redeeming God; if He does not choose to heal my depression, can He use it in redeeming ways? Can I trust that His work is redemptive, even when I may never in my lifetime understand how?*

I returned to prayer.

I give it up, Lord. Take my husband, take my children, take my heart longing for their well-being—take it all. You love them better than I can. Forgive me for forgetting this.

Oh, Lord, I still long to be well, but I will surrender that desire to You.

How to Do It All
by Gina Martin

I can't do it all. As hard as I try, I can't be the perfect wife and mother. I can't grow all my own food, cook from scratch, bake my own bread, and preserve all the food we need for winter. I can't have beautiful flower beds and an immaculate home with meticulously organized closets, ready to host guests at any moment. I can't be the first to volunteer for any church ministry, sew lovely clothing for my family, do fun art projects with my children, and have time left for my husband. I can't scrapbook, knit, embroider, quilt, and all the other things I can try to squeeze into my days. Yes, I can do some of these things some of the time, but not all these things all the time. And never can I accomplish all that I thought was possible in the freshness of the morning. Each day when my husband comes home, he asks me about my day, and I reply, "I didn't get it all done."

Of course, I know I can't do it all. In my head I know it. But I don't live like I believe it. Somehow I think that if I would be a little more efficient, work a little faster, or wake up earlier, I can "get it all done." So I read another homemaking book, search for one more tip on time efficiency, and buy another organizational gizmo touted to give me more time. I keep dreaming that after canning season is over, or I finish some sewing, or the holidays pass, then life will slow down and I'll have time for everything.

It is a lie. I already have far too many interests, projects, and plain old work for several lifetimes. I'm not condoning laziness—just realizing I need to face reality. And today, my reality is a houseful of little ones that need fed, clothed, trained, and taught—by me.

Why do I end every day in frustration over how many things are still undone? Everything I did today—cooking, laundry, cleaning—will need done again tomorrow. And there was much more I *wanted* to do that I was forced to omit.

So I finally admit it: I can't do it all. Why did it take so long? Am I attempting too much? Or trying to be someone I am not? Probing deeper in my heart I find that I have placed homemaking on a pedestal where it did not belong. I want to appear to be a perfect woman. But instead of appearing good in the sight of others, the purpose of everything I do should be glorifying God. God in His sovereignty has given me all the time, energy, and resources I need to do His will. His will—not my wishes.

None of my circumstances come as a surprise to God but are allowed by Him for my good. God cares about my frustrations but He is more concerned about my spiritual growth in the midst of these trials, than that I "get it all done." When I am discontent with my circumstances, I am complaining that the One who plans my life has made a mistake. If I can't get it all done, either I am attempting to do more than God wants me to, or God has other plans for my time. Today, did I love God with all my heart, soul, mind, and strength? Did I love my neighbor as myself? If I can say "yes" to those questions, does it really matter if my kitchen floor didn't get mopped?

How do I break a mindset where success is found in accomplishment and where a good day is measured by the checks on the to-do list? I believe God is waiting for me to repent of putting my own glory above His. He wants me to ask for His out-pouring of grace to help me serve others instead of feeding my own desire to feel successful. *"According as his divine power hath given unto us all things that pertain unto life and godliness, through the knowledge of him that hath called us to glory and virtue." (2 Peter 1:3)*

Maybe the next time my husband asks "How was your day?" I shouldn't interpret it to mean "Did you *get it all done*?" Maybe instead I need to ask myself "How did today's challenges bring maturity in my life and glorify the Lord?" Maybe then my heart can be filled with praise to my Heavenly Father who considers my growth in holiness more important than clean floors. Maybe then I can worship instead of stress. Even on the busiest of days.

And with worship, my day can be successful, even when *I can't do it all*. Because when I have my priorities right, when worship is first, I **can** *do it all*. Not all I want to do, but all that God has called me to do. And therein lies the difference.

Choicest Blessing
by Lydia Hess

As she viewed the stately towers,
An array of zinnia flowers,
My young daughter chose a few to pick—for me!
"Pink's my favorite kind," she said,
"And my favorite kind is red.
And it's orange," she blurted out bewilderedly.

As I reap a full bouquet
Of God's blessings day by day,
I am overwhelmed by what He's given me;
Though I know my favorite one
Is the token of God's Son,
For through Him, my blessings last eternally.

In the Garden
by Stephanie J. Leinbach

We raced against the sunset, robins squabbling in the pines over their night roosts, fireflies rising from the grass with lanterns flaring.

Pausing to straighten and unkink his back, my husband said, "I remember pulling weeds when I was young."

I looked at him across the rows of knee-high corn. "Did you complain about it like I did?"

"Well, actually, I remember thinking I couldn't wait until I grew up, so I wouldn't have to pull weeds."

I laughed. "Then what are you doing out here?"

"Pulling weeds," he muttered, getting back to work. "I can plow and plant, no problem, but I will never like this part of gardening."

Our girls, newly freed from weeding duties, burst out from under a nearby pine tree, tiny cones piled in their hands. "Who wants to buy pine cones?" the five year old asked. "They cost $50.00."

"$50.00!" I yanked at a stubborn weed. "That's too much money for me."

"What about $5.00?" She looked hopeful.

"Sure, but I don't have my wallet."

"I have it." She waved an imaginary wallet. "I'll take $5.00 out of it." She wandered over to her father. "Do you want some money, Dad?"

"No, I don't want any money right now." He tossed a handful of weeds down. "Do you know what I really want from you?"

She didn't hesitate. "Obedience," she said and shot beneath the pine tree before her declaration was tested.

Her word hung in the air, and I pulled more weeds to its echo.

Obedience. What I really want from you.

I sat back on my heels, dusting off my hands, and watched the light fade behind Brush Mountain. *Obedience. It's what You really want from me, God. Remind me again of Your commands.*

Gently, the Word unfolded in my heart: *Love God with all thy heart. In everything give thanks. Pray without ceasing.*

I winced. Truth hurts.

Wives, submit. Rejoice evermore. Love thy neighbor as thyself.

The unchanging Word washed over my weary soul. I was convicted and renewed all at once.

Laughing and shrieking, the girls raced past me, caught up in another invented game. "Come, girls," I called, getting to my feet. "It's time for baths and bed."

As I herded my little flock toward the house, I pondered the life-changing power of simple obedience. Simple, but so hard.

Do you know what I really want from you? His voice still probed my heart.

Obedience, Lord.

I drew a deep breath of the growing darkness, watching the girls chasing fireflies, dancing with arms outstretched to the starry heavens. *Thank You, Lord.*

My husband fell into step beside me. "Why are you smiling?" he asked.

I looked from the girls to him, gratefulness warming my heart. "I just realized God likes to teach lessons on obedience in a garden."

Is Being a Good Mom Good Enough?

by Stephanie J. Leinbach

The alarm clock glowed midnight when I crawled into bed, my newborn son finally asleep in his bassinet. I burrowed into the covers, seeking comfort, seeking sleep.

My husband rolled over. "Thanks for being a good mom," he said, his voice foggy with sleep.

His words startled me. He who sleeps through nearly everything awoke to say this? I huffed—in laughter, in surprise, I'm not sure which. "In what way do you mean?" Why do I question every compliment?

"You take care of him." He sounded exasperated, as if it should have been obvious. In the startled silence that followed, his breathing deepened and slowed.

I blinked at the ceiling, remembering my manners too late. "Thank you," I said to his oblivious form.

Tired as I was, sleep should have come quickly, but I lay awake, cradling his words to my heart: *Thanks for being a good mom.*

Life had been topsy-turvy lately. At times, the demands of motherhood overwhelmed me, made me doubt my ability to handle it with grace and patience. Could I do it? Hardly. I failed so often.

Every day, I worried I wasn't doing enough for my family. I felt guilty when I couldn't keep after my responsibilities. I lay awake on nights such as these, weary to the bone, and remembered all the times I should have spoken more gently, acted more kindly, smiled more frequently.

But he thought I was a good mom.

Is it enough to be a good mom? And while I was thinking about it, what does a good mom do? Lying in the dark, I held up that last question and scrutinized it.

It wasn't hard to answer.

A good mom follows God and obeys His commands.

A good mom respects her husband and seeks to please him.

A good mom loves her children and takes care of them.

Christian mothers are required to shoulder these three responsibilities regardless of who they are and where they live. Beyond these three, I could name many other duties and expectations, but they were cultural demands placed upon me because I'm an American Mennonite housewife, not because I'm a mother. These expectations are activities such as housecleaning every spring and fall; canning pickles, jams, and five types of tomato sauces; gardening; baking bread; and keeping every closet, drawer, and cupboard organized. Yes, it would be nice to do all these things, to be efficient and self-sufficient, to be always caught up and kept after—but if I do these things, I am being a good seamstress, gardener, organizer, baker, and housewife. None of these activities mean I'm being a good mom, no matter what my Mennonite culture might otherwise say.

Not that there's anything wrong with these activities. Many good moms are—for example—excellent gardeners and bakers. But my success as a mother is not dependent upon my ability to raise magnificent vegetables or decorate elaborate birthday cakes. I do not have to excel at everything to be a good mom.

Being a good mom is not complicated, but I tend to make it so. I obsess over the many details of living and play internal comparison games with other mothers' accomplishments and grow discouraged with my inadequacies. I need to stop it.

You know what my problem is? I don't want to be a good mom. I want to be a perfect mom. I want to do it right and do it all and do it so that others are impressed with my ability to train my children and keep my house. I want perfection. Being good isn't good enough.

No wonder I get discouraged.

My pursuit of perfect motherhood is not only impossible, but it is also rooted in pride and must be yanked from my heart. In its place, I need to plant the seeds of humility, service, and contentment.

When I climb into bed each night, I need to ask myself: *Did I follow God today? Did I respect my husband? Did I love my children?* If I can say yes to these questions, then my day was a success.

I will have been a good mom, and that is good enough.

ESSENCE OF LIFE
by MJZ

The wrinkled hand holds the tiny one.
The nearly done and the just begun,
The very old and the very young.
'Tis the course of life, so short, so long.
The white head bends to the wee one fair
And the essence of time is captured there.

A portrait of life in a glance is seen—
The aged, the babe—and the years between.
The dawn meets dusk, and their beauty glows.
Together—the bud and the fading rose.
Both rest in the hands of the God unseen—
The young—and the old—and the years between.

LOST!
by Regena L. Weaver

Not so very long ago we were given a petite pink bundle. We adored this bit of humanity with all the ardour of first-time parents. We loved her dark "sunrise eyes" and the quirky folded ear (a newborn's souvenir of the too-cramped womb). We smothered her with cuddles and kisses.

We "fought" (good-naturedly, of course) for the privilege of holding her in church . . . and a little less willingly carried her in the wee hours of the morning. All the high ideals of new parents were imposed on this wee one. Each new accomplishment was celebrated and recognized as the miracle it was. Almost overnight (a mostly sleepless one) she became a loquacious toddler who delighted in embarrassing and amazing her parents by turns.

But something happened. We lost her! Sometimes I see hints of her around. In the "sunrise eyes" behind the purple spectacles of the young lady curled up with *Sandy's Anchor of Hope*.

In the vivid imagination that reveals itself in the stories being told by the fourth-grader, reminiscent of the loquacious toddler of yesterday.

We used to have a fat dream-baby with black hair, too. Where did he go? Someone may have mistaken him for an Eskimo and sent him north. We loved the pudgy rolls of that nearly-newborn, as well as the slimmed-down older version that was soon cruising around. But he's gone! I used to be able to track him down by looking for the pants he crawled out of, and the garbage cans he overturned. But my kitchen garbage can stands mutely in the corner and there are no size 6-9-month blue jeans in sight.

And while the kidnapper Time was around he must have taken the pink whirlwind with the mop of dark hair, too. I was leery of something happening to her, and I thought I was keeping a close eye on her. In fact, once I thought I had lost her, but she was just up on a chest of drawers in our bedroom, playing with straight pins. We built a fence to try to contain this little lass with wings on her feet. The fence is still there, but the little whirlwind has escaped.

I don't especially mind the loss of all the laundry generated by the long-limbed lad with the reflux problem, but I'd love to cuddle his petite body and look deep into his wise eyes. With his wispy bit of blonde hair he was a complete surprise, but we couldn't disown a baby who looked exactly like his Grandpa! The blonde wisps and reflux problems are gone, but I get reminders of the wise-eyed lad when I look into the face of my son and try to satisfy his "Whys."

The petite baby with the "sunrise eyes," the dream-baby with the straight black hair, the wee lass with the twinkle toes, and the long-limbed lad with the knowing eyes . . . if anyone finds these treasures please return them to me. I miss them.

Only one thing bothers me . . . my lap is already full. A winsome cherub with a single dimple and a nose that scrunches up when she smiles has taken up residence there.

Maybe, after all, it's best to treasure memories and put my energies into tending this dimpled cherub and her four doting babysitters . . . the young lady with the "sunrise eyes," the creative dark-haired boy, the energetic lass, and the inquisitive lad with the wise eyes.

Messy Morning
by Sarah Martin

Today was one of those mornings when by 8:00 I could have sat down and indulged in a good cry, and for sure by 8:45—my twelve year old sassed back at me for various things and left a trail of tears among his siblings; my ten year old was uncharacteristically unkind to her younger sister; my eight year old was as dense as a donkey about some snack crackers for his lunch; my five year old whined and wouldn't obey when I gave a command; and my three year old got mad at the breakfast table because he wanted more vitamins than was his share. The baby was good as gold while her older brothers "tested her balance and reflexes" and altered her facial expressions but then cried the entire time I was dressing her, while the preschoolers squabbled over a coloring book.

I hate feeling glad to send my scholars out the door but this morning I did. I can't help but wonder, though, how their school day goes after a morning like this. *Does the general mood of chaos follow them and make it hard to be cheerful? Were they glad to get away from me? What kind of mom am I anyway, who can't control her children and by calm words change the air from suppressed eruption to one of cheerfulness and respect? Why did God give me six? Where did I miss it? What am I doing wrong?* These are the thoughts that plague me after the door swings shut for the last time on three children heading to school and I sit down to feed my sleepy baby.

Here is where Satan will quickly get a foothold. I can indulge the whispers of "You're sure not a good mom"; "How come you don't have more respect than that?"; "When are you going to get that 'cheerful obedience' thing downpat?"

Or, I can choose to call up that still, small Voice in my heart, the one I've been trying desperately to keep in touch with while the messy moments swirl around me. Now that the house is quiet, I can hear Him better, if I let myself . . . "Be not weary in well doing"; "He shall . . . gently lead those that are with young"; "For line must be upon line, line upon line, precept upon precept; here a little and there a little." Sometimes my problem is that I want my children to be all good, right now! But if they never misbehaved, the realistic truth is that I would never have opportunities to teach. And if I judge my identity by my children's performance, I forget that if my children "turn out" it will be in spite of me, not because of me. God is at work here, and I can but try to be a faithful ground-work layer.

And really, I think my children will have a good day of school (they have great teachers). The baby is peacefully having a nap and I plant a feather-light kiss on her cherry blossom cheek. The preschoolers are agreeably visiting while they enjoy a snack of crackers and juice on the kitchen floor. When the scholars get home they'll be in a good frame of mind and the morning's grief will have faded. Hmm . . . I really do have pretty normal children after all. And with Jesus ministering to my heart, I remember that they are also absolutely precious. Their faults are part of being human, immature human at that! And with another faulty human for a mom, we can expect some chaotic mornings.

But with a patient Heavenly Father for a teacher, we can also expect calm after the storm.

On Mother's Day
by Crystal Steinhauer

It was my second Mother's Day—the day when all my labors for everyone's health and happiness would be rewarded. Would my husband give me a card, flowers perhaps, tell me what a good mother I am to our two little girls, or—oh, rapture—help with the dinner dishes?

Arriving home from church, we pulled into our driveway, and Davy helped Tasha out of her car seat. They disappeared around the corner of the house and I lingered in the car, enjoying the balmy day a little longer. Father and daughter reappeared, daughter carrying a mismatched bouquet—a few tulips, an iris, and a bluebell. The sweetest little Mother's Day flowers anyone has received.

My husband lifted the infant seat out of the car. I grabbed the diaper bag and stack of church mail and we headed inside. The kitchen reminded me that even Mother's Day can have its imperfections. I hadn't gotten up early enough and the breakfast dishes resting on the table testified of it. Muffins, drying out in their tins, lounged on the counter. But the roast simmering in the crock pot smelled delicious. The potatoes and carrots were soft. The elder daughter was still running around saying, "Pick flowers," and the younger was fast asleep in her car seat.

Now, if Davy would clear off the breakfast dishes and set the table, I could make some gravy and lunch would be ready in no time. Then maybe if he helped me with dishes afterward, we'd have time to take some mother/daughter pictures before I put the girls down for naps.

I tried to pour the broth out of the crock pot, but failed, potatoes and carrots jostling to be first. Where was Davy? I glanced back at the table, annoyed to see it untouched and my husband nowhere in sight. I peeked in the living room. He was stretched out on the couch, reading. I suppose he hadn't thought of it that a little help in the kitchen would be nice, especially on Mother's Day.

"Can you help me pour the broth into the kettle?" I asked. He came willingly.

I rolled my eyes at the table. "And it would be nice if you'd set the table."

Tasha trundled over to her baby sister's car seat and jerked the blanket off. "Baby Zoe sleeping," she said. Not anymore. Two eyelids popped open. Her blue eyes peered about the kitchen before she started wailing.

I whisked the flour paste desperately, but the lumps were destined to stay. I shrugged and poured it into the broth. And where had Davy gone, anyway? He was done setting the table. Couldn't he hear the baby crying?

I jerked a knife from the block and sliced homemade bread to the rhythm of wails. Davy reappeared and took Zoe out of her seat, and then used his free hand to put Tasha in her high chair. "Say, 'We're hungry, Mommy,'" he said.

The little parrot said, "Hungry, Mommy!"

I squelched my irritation and plopped strawberry jelly beside the bread. "Where's the butter?" That was one lucky stroke from not getting breakfast put away—the butter should be nice and soft from sitting out all morning.

"The butter?" Davy said. "I put it in the fridge." Of course.

I carried the crock pot to the table and was ready to sit down when I thought of it. "I forgot the asparagus. Shall I cook it quickly?"

"Sure," Davy said.

I pulled a kettle from the drawer and ran water into it, dropping the vegetable in and adding a little salt.

"Let it cook. We can pray a while," Davy suggested.

I joined my family and we prayed—what did we pray? Probably "God Is Great," because that's what we nearly always pray.

"Water. Water. Water," Tasha crowed. I picked up her cup. Empty. Shouldn't the table setter have thought of that?

I leaped up, filled it, and returned to the table. The asparagus! It was cooked to a mushy olive green. Just how I like it least.

I cut up Tasha's meat, mashed her potato, and diced her carrots. "Soup," she said approvingly as I blopped lumpy gravy over everything. I got the baby settled nursing and then started on my own food. Davy was already half done.

"I'm tired of being a mom," I said. "I need a vacation."

He looked surprised. "On Mother's Day? This is supposed to be the day when you love being a mom the most!"

Maybe if I wouldn't be so overworked and underappreciated, I thought.

Lunch over, I faced the dreary pile of dishes. Alone. Childish laughter came from the living room where Tasha played with her daddy. *Sounds like fun. Of course I won't get any help with the dishes.*

Stop. Enough of your selfishness. Enough of wanting to be babied just because it's Mother's Day. What was different about today than other Sundays? Many Sundays things didn't go perfectly and even more Sundays I did the dishes alone. Why was this Sunday different?

"Today is Mother's Day," I told the smeared dishes. "I'm taking a break." I turned my back on the kitchen.

"Mommy!" Tasha cheered as I joined them on the couch. She crawled onto my lap. "Book," she said, dragging *Dick and Jane* off the end table. Next to us, Zoe cooed in response to her dad's tickle. This is where I belong. These are the people I love most.

It was Mother's Day and I had a choice. I could nurture my disappointment and let it ruin my day or I could look beyond my unfulfilled expectations and forgive them for not noticing that I'd like a little bit of extra coddling.

And after I put the girls to bed for their naps and spent some quality time with my husband, I returned to the kitchen to tackle those dishes—and sang as I scrubbed—on Mother's Day.

---

by Faith Sommers

Every home needs a four or five year old. It's just so nice to have someone to run those little errands around the house and yard.

We had a nearly five-year space between two of the children, and the five year old was busily working on his preschool books to prepare for first grade.

The baby was only that—a baby. He couldn't hang out laundry, much less fold the clothes, get me a drink, find a diaper or a blanket, sweep behind the couch where I couldn't reach . . . and all the myriads of other little jobs that need doing.

I watched the preschooler's eyes light up when we purchased a lunch box for school. And sighed—my thoughts becoming words, "What will I do without your help?"

His smile faded just a bit, then he said solemnly, "You'll just have to work more."

Applesauce and the Blame Game
by Gina Martin

I was in a frantic scramble to turn apples into sauce before anymore rotted. The clock was ticking, my time limited, and each movement needed to count.

A row of jars stood on the counter, awaiting lids. As I stretched to reach over the jars, one jar toppled. Applesauce splashed across the counter, down my dress, dripping to the floor.

I looked quickly for broken glass and grabbed a towel to stop any further mess. Although grateful to find the jar unbroken, I found myself looking around in irritation.

But I was alone. No one was in the kitchen but me. With shock, I realized I was searching for someone to blame. I shudder to think what words would have escaped if the usual bevy of children had been at my elbow. I heard their happy voices playing in a nearby room. This time, there was nothing but my own clumsiness to blame.

For the next several hours, while washing apples, stirring pots, squeezing sauce, and scrubbing pans, I had much to ponder. How often do I lash out at my helpers when an accident happens? Do I always blame others in times of difficulty, big or small? Do I never stop to consider that maybe I am the one to blame?

The reaction is as old as our Grandmother Eve. I blame the serpent. The children You gave me. My husband. Or the house, the weather, my aching back, the economy, her, him, them, it . . . endless the things, people, and circumstances at the focus of my anger.

What if I turned my accusing finger inward? If I said, "I have sinned. I was impatient. I knocked over the jar. I spoke unkindly. Please forgive me." Would my heart then be lighter, the burden lifted? If I turned my frustrations into songs of joy, would I find the "joy of the Lord is my strength?" Could I carry my burden, the endless tasks, the time limits, the uncomfortable circumstances to my Father and there find the promised rest?

Some days it seems impossible to find the time to sit at Jesus' feet, this needful thing that Mary chose. But I can choose to spend time in His Word and tune my heart to His voice. If I want to stop blaming my circumstances, I need to start working on the person I can change.

Then when applesauce spills, may only loving words escape.

Peace in the Midst of Sandy
by Regina Rosenberry

The bathtubs are filled. The 5-gallon Igloo is full. The lantern's oil is replenished and milk and bread are stocked. Let the hurricane come; we are ready.

And so she comes, howling up from the hollows and hitting the house with all her pent-up fury. But the children are home from school, my husband home from work and supper is on the table. I'm praising God in my heart that all is snug and safe.

Then, the phone rings. It's a desperate farmer. A wire has been torn down by a falling tree branch and the cows must be milked. Can my husband—an electrician by trade—please come?

I plead for him to stay at home but duty calls. I hear his truck leave amidst the pelting of rain and hail on the windows. My heart trembles. Hurricane Sandy has picked up speed and the wind is now the furious wolf trying to blow our house down. My husband will need to work in his bucket truck high on top an electric pole, and I begin to imagine the worst.

The lights of his truck just fade from sight when our own houselights flicker. And blink. And flicker. Then out, and all is dark. The four year old begins to cry in fear and clutch my skirt; my heart whimpers with her.

But my son joyfully brings the flashlight and we light the lanterns. Okay, so maybe this can be fun. I look around to see what I can do to entertain the children and to keep my thoughts from its constant worry for my husband's safety. And then I see it. Songbooks—of course! One thing in the house that didn't take electricity. We could sing.

So my son sets the lantern on the table. The crying four year old's sniffle stops as she joins in singing a children's song. And then my oldest daughter suggests, "Blessed Quietness." I hum the soprano note while my son gets the tenor and my daughter takes the alto. Into this old hymn we go, and as the words unfold from our lips, my heart is amazed at the song my daughter chose.

> "Blessed quietness, holy quietness,
> blest assurance in my soul.
> On the stormy sea Jesus speaks to me,
> and the billows cease to roll!"

Outside, the wind continued to howl, but the billows in my heart were now quiet and still. Jesus had spoken, and there was peace.

Thank you, Jesus!

Refocus
by Sue Hooley

For 17 months we rented a two-story century-old house on 1/16 of an acre beside a Safeway grocery store. We became accustomed to living in town, but we are country folks and we didn't learn to enjoy the sound of grocery carts rolling across the pavement. Neither did we get used to hearing voices at any hour of the night or the ear-piercing fire sirens.

We eagerly searched for a place to buy in the country and finally we settled on 21 acres of bare land. This would be the third move in less than two years and we were longing to be settled. We promptly built a barn to accommodate future animals. We ordered a custom triple-wide manufactured house and after it was set, a garage, office and breezeway were added to the house.

We loved our new location, but reality has a way of becoming real. Every time I looked outside I saw mega dirt piles. Seed catalogs were tantalizing because there wasn't a garden plot and farm magazines were a reminder that the barn was unfinished. Everywhere I turned there were projects large and small that needed to be done. Typically, developing a piece of property takes *more* time and *more* money than anticipated and our project was no exception.

One day after discussing dwindling building funds I went to the garage to retrieve a package of ground beef from the freezer. There at the base of the freezer lay the head of a prize mole that the cat had graciously deposited for my viewing. "Oh, yuck!" I gasped. *If only we had garage doors the cats couldn't even come in here*! In desperation I prayed, "Lord, help me to be patient and please send us $20,000."

An icy fear gripped me when I thought of ways of how that prayer could be quickly answered. My husband could be seriously injured and we might receive gifts of charity. One of my children could die in an automobile accident and liability insurance money might be given to us. *Did I really want a quick-fix to the inconveniences that faced me?*

Mole heads, dirt piles and the lack of garage doors seemed insignificant as I considered my hasty, foolish prayer. "Lord, it's alright, we'll work through this and please cancel my very selfish request." As I took a few minutes to refocus, I thought of things I was enjoying for which I hadn't paid a dime: We were having an excellent school year and my third and seventh grade sons were sorry that it was rapidly coming to an end. The youth group had just had a profitable discussion on stewardship. Our church is experiencing a time of peace and we had just had a meaningful communion service. The need for finances still existed, but my demanding attitude went through a modification process.

The synonyms for the word "development" are "progress" and "growth." In my frustration the only synonyms that I could think of were "dirt piles," "saw dust," and "endless decisions." When I was able to look factually at the development project in terms of progress and growth, the whole situation looked more hopeful.

When I was a young mother, my mother-in-law told me about a mother who was extremely tired of washing diapers. The mother thoughtlessly said, "I wouldn't care if I never washed another diaper." My mother-in-law cautioned, "Be careful what you say when you are weary, you could lose your children much faster than they were born to you."

The synonyms for infant are: "baby," "newborn" and "nursling." That gives the impression of a small, helpless person that needs a lot of care. After a few sleepless nights, a new set of synonyms can appear like "dirty diapers," "interrupted schedules" and "fatigue." Learning to separate the frustration from what is causing it can help you to refocus. You are only tired of the weariness, not tired of the baby. It becomes easy to say something rash when we are weary and frustrated. On the other side, it may be healthy to prudently acknowledge that the nights are tough and your emotions are unsteady.

In Judges 11, Jepthah was preparing to fight the Ammonites. The job ahead looked insurmountable and in his desperation he told the Lord, "If You deliver the children of Ammon into my hands then I will sacrifice whatever comes out of my house to meet me when I return home." The Ammonites were conquered and his daughter met him at the door. Jepthah was a man of his word and a few months later, he sorrowfully sacrificed his daughter. God didn't require Jepthah to make such a hasty vow to accomplish victory. No doubt a simple request to the Lord for help in fighting the Ammonites would have produced the same results.

When we are in the middle of an intense situation, it is normal to respond to our feelings. It is not wrong to have feelings of frustration, but it is dangerous to react on those feelings. When we are under pressure it is easy to say words that we may later regret.

The Bible gives some practical advice on developing ways of dealing with frustrations, and our almighty God truly cares about every aspect of our lives. "***Call** upon the LORD*, who is worthy to be praised." (Psalm 18:3a) "***Wait** upon the LORD* [He] shall renew [your] strength." (Isaiah 40:31a) **Remember:** All things work together for good to them that love God. (Roman 8:28a)

Intense situations are often temporary and, like dirt piles, they will disappear with time and effort. If you take a moment to **call, wait** and **remember**, likely your focus will change and God will bless you for trusting in Him. "For the eyes of the LORD run to and fro throughout the whole earth, to shew himself strong in the behalf of them whose heart is perfect toward him." (2 Chronicles 16:9)

Squirrel for Snack, Anyone?
by Sarah Martin

"Mom!" My vivacious seven year old burst into the house. "I need a paring knife! Edward Dale shot a squirrel with the BB gun and we're gonna skin it, then fry it and eat it! I need a knife to help skin!" He hopped from one foot to the other, fairly oozing vitality and excitement.

Shudders. "One of my good paring knives?"

"Yes! Pleeease? Darin and Edward Dale have their jack knives but I don't have one."

I guess I could always boil it when they're done. "Okay, you may have this one," I replied, trying to hide my reluctance as I handed it over.

"Thanks!" he flung over his shoulder as he leaped back out onto the porch and closed the door with a bang, all in one motion.

Their brother's excited voice had gotten the girls' attention and they were soon hovering over the little porch table, following the proceedings with interest. I stepped out, too, enjoying the warm sunshine as I observed the activity. Big brother Edward Dale took the first turn to skin, while Kenton and cousin Darin each grasped a tiny back leg and splayed them wide, "to make the hide come off easier. This is how Uncle Ben skins deer."

"Mom, get a frying pan ready!" Edward Dale instructed.

Not one of mine! "Are you sure . . . ? How will you prepare it? How do you even know squirrel meat is good to eat?" I asked.

"Oh, it is. Daniel's boys have eaten it already. We'll just . . . fry it, or something. In lots of butter." He looked at me confidently.

My mind was going 90 miles an hour. I don't want to discourage them from trying new things . . . but a squirrel's a varmint! Who knows what it ate? "What if you don't cook it well enough and someone gets a tummy ache?" I asked, hoping they would change their minds.

"Come on, Mom. We'll fry it really good. It won't hurt us."

I wonder. "I'll heat the frying pan when you're done getting it ready." I relented.

I stepped back into the house, trying to be excited for the boys. I told myself they would be just fine, that many a pioneer ate stranger things than squirrel, that I don't want to be the hovering kind of mom that's afraid to let her boys be boys. Besides, they were so excited!

Fifteen minutes later, Kenton was back. "Mom, where's some coarse salt? We're not going to eat this one after all, but I want to tan the hide."

I tried to hide my relief and casually answered, "Okay. Here, this is some salt left over from when we made ice cream last time. Bring the box back in when you're done with it."

"Yup!" and he was gone again.

A few days later, the boys brought the little grey-brown pelt to me. "Feel this, Mom. It's so soft." Yeah, and it's probably full of lice and who-knows-what. I stroked the furry article, and had to admit, it was undeniably silky. "Pretty," I murmured. "Are you . . . keeping this up in your room? Like, isn't it germy?"

"Oh, no, Mom! It's clean! Plus, the salt preserved it and it's so nice." They were so confident. I didn't say more. I wish they'd just take it to the shop and keep it out there. But the little pelt stayed in the boys' room and eventually I stopped imagining lice crawling from it every time I saw it.

• • • • •

Several weeks later, however, the inevitable happened. The boys burst in the door. "Mom, where's the frying pan? We got another squirrel and we skinned it already. We're gonna fry the drumsticks for you and Dad! We know exactly how because the other day when we were at Uncle Ben's he helped us do some. It's terrible good!

"Okay, first we need lots of butter . . . Mom, you go out of the kitchen while we do it, okay? This is our treat for you!" My twelve-year-old's eyes sparkled warmly into mine. It was a rare moment. I smiled back and went to the next room. But I couldn't resist calling back, "Make sure it's fried really well!"

"Oh, we will, don't worry! It's going to be so good you won't be able to believe it. Now. Kenton . . ." He loved to be in charge. I decided to deliberately enjoy the sounds and smells from the kitchen, as the pan began to sizzle merrily and spicy smells wafted past my nose.

Sure enough, in a few minutes, my sons came proudly to where I sat at the table, bearing on a tiny china plate two miniature "drumsticks," well-fried and crispy. "Thanks, boys," I said, picking one up. I refused to notice the singed little hairs clinging to the morsel of meat, and winged a prayer, hardly more than a breath, "Keep me safe from this meat if there's anything dangerous about it." My eager sons hovered near as I raised it to my mouth. "Is it good?" they asked hopefully before I even took a bite. "It tastes like chicken, doesn't it?"

At that moment, I had a flash of clarity. This was all about relationships. That I enjoyed my treat was extremely important to my sons. So I would enjoy it. I bit into the snack with a delightful crunch. "It's very good," I assured the boys. And I meant it. It was. And even better than the flavor was the thought that they had wanted to do this for me; it was something special and they wanted to share it. If I want them to come to me with their troubles and secrets in some distant future day, I need to enter into the moment now and build the relationship I want to stand me in good stead then.

I smiled into the eyes of my dear sons. "Yes, this is good. You need to go find Dad and make sure he gets one while they're hot. I think he'll like it, too."

"Lest We Forget"
by L. D. Nolt

I was given a very provoking thought by an older woman of wisdom a few days ago. We were talking about mothers and why it seems that so often we hear of women being discouraged and overwhelmed with life. This woman said to me, "I wouldn't want to raise children now. The standard for Moms is too high."

As I thought about this it became more and more of a truth to me. But why? Why is the standard higher now than it was back when she was raising children? The more I thought about it the more I realized that it is that way because we allow it to be.

As the world drifts farther and farther from God and from holiness, have we been following, albeit, at a slower pace? We work hard at keeping our places neat and looking good. We also work very hard at appearances. Our children we clothe in neatness, possibly even stylishness and make sure they lack nothing. Our vehicles we also need to be not only dependable but sharp looking and clean.

None of those things are wrong in themselves. We have a duty to present neatness and cleanliness to those around us. We are duty bound to take proper care of our families and our properties. Otherwise how can we be approachable or have lifestyles that look attractive to the world? But how much of what we do is based on pride or on other people's expectations?

It is sobering to me to think that because of having to "keep up with the Joneses" so to speak, we cannot only harm ourselves mentally and emotionally but also spiritually. You may think, like

I did, that "I'm fine, I don't really have a problem keeping up with the crowd." But then I got to thinking a bit . . .

What about all the money spent on keeping ourselves up with the neighbors or the "standard?" What about the things around the house we do that wouldn't necessarily be done? What about making sure that my children match perfectly, maybe seeking after name-brand clothing instead of simply looking neat? What about my house? Decorations? Toys? How much do I do for appearances?

It did me good to consider if I would really do all those things as faithfully as I do if it wouldn't be for what other people might think of me if I didn't. Again, not that these things are necessarily wrong, but what is my motive for doing them? Am I willing to cut back when I need to for the sake of my family, even if it may mean not having things as nice as the neighbors, but keep me available and healthy mentally, emotionally, and spiritually?

Do I unknowingly make things harder for someone else because I spend so much time focusing on things that are so material? I am then setting a standard that may not only be harmful to me but also to someone else.

These verses in Deuteronomy 6:10-12 are sobering: "And it shall be, when the LORD thy God shall have brought thee into the land which he swore unto thy fathers, to Abraham, to Isaac, and to Jacob, to give thee great and goodly cities, which thou buildedst not, And houses full of all good things, which thou filledst not, and wells digged, which thou diggedst not, vineyards and olive trees, which thou plantedst not; when thou shalt have eaten and be full; Then beware lest thou forget the LORD, which brought thee forth out of the land of Egypt, from the house of bondage."

Have we fallen into the trap of busyness to the point of neglecting ourselves and our families? Maybe I don't even recognize it because it is what I have always done. But it is good to stop every now and then and evaluate our situation.

Am I continually frustrated? Short with my husband and children? Do I rarely get enough time to spend with my Lord? Do I struggle with feeling down when I am around others because I want what they have; clothes, vehicles, nice houses, vacations? Do I cause my husband financial hardships because I am determined to "keep up with the rest?"

What about recognizing my weaknesses? Do I take time to apologize for my wrongs so I don't continually repeat those hurts to my family? Or am I so busy I don't realize the harm I am causing as I bulldoze my way through my day?

Where does our worth come from? Is it in how much we accomplish? Does God love us by how much work we get done? I am amazed how God's love is perfect, unchanging, and boundless. My worth lies only in HIS love for me!

If I mess up, His love is there. If others think I'm strange or a failure, His love is still there. If I do good, His love is no greater. If others think I have it all together, His love is still the same. I don't need to do anything to merit His love. If I was the worst sinner or the best saint, His love is the same to me. Therein, lies my worth.

Who am I pleasing? God or others? What is my goal in life? Should it not be to do God's will? Why would God's will be to have ourselves and places look perfect? "That others may see our good works and glorify our Father in Heaven . . ." Does having our places "perfect" do that? I think if we focus on God's will for our lives, things like having our places neat as a pin, fade away.

There is always work to do. But our children, our husbands, our family and friends, even this earthly life, will not always be here. We have so much and have been blessed but beware, lest we forget God!

We can stop the cycle of continued busyness and instead pass on to our children the things in life that really matter. Things like time spent together, stopping to enjoy the flowers, a nest of baby birdies, the laughter of a swing ride especially when being pushed by Mommy, relaxing after a hard day's work, a job well done, a book read together, shared Bible reading, working together, laughing together, praying together and so much more.

We should also recognize whether a lot of the reason we spent so much time on appearances of ourselves and our properties and families may really be rooted in pride. Psalm 10:4 says, "The wicked, through the pride of his countenance, will not seek after God: God is not in all his thoughts." What a sad situation.

I realize as I write this that I have failed in this area many times. I like when things look nice, I love having beautiful flower beds and a country decorated house; though that may not be wrong, I sometimes get so caught up in that fact that I won't invite friends over or be hospitable because my place "doesn't look good enough." I tend to agonize over what to wear on my children or myself when I go certain places because I want to appear "put together." And in focusing so much on those things I become frustrated and my family suffers.

And what is the root of the problem? Pride.

I pray that you will join me in breaking the cycle of material perfection and that together we can strive for spiritual perfection with the help of God.

In all of life's responsibility, beware lest we forget the Lord our God!!

My Reality
by Meredith Horst

We've all read about them. Stories, poems, articles about mothers. Morning sickness, weary pregnancies, long labors. Positive pregnancy tests, the first flutters within, the exuberance of the birth finally over. Tiny newborns, a row of preschoolers, five schoolchildren. We like to read about mothers.

And then there's me. I never had, never did, never saw, never felt any of these things. But I'm a mother. Phone calls, mountains of paperwork, background checks. Required reading, first aid and CPR training, proof of income. I know about these. Social workers, attorneys, judges. I spoke to these. They helped us to become parents, me to become a mother.

Adoption—a miracle, an act of our God to redeem bad situations. A needy child and empty arms—God brings them together. Only God can cause a mother to conceive. Only God could bring a baby, this baby out of many born in a gigantic city on the other side of the world to our home in rural Kentucky. Only God could make me a mother.

I was surprised at how soon after we were married I started to wish for a baby. Of course the baby was going to come from our bodies. But one day months later, the doctor gave us the verdict. There would be no babies. Numbness, shock, raw grief, tears, a hole in our hearts, a physical ache in my arms. We had our turn with all of these.

But God was still there, and He ministered to us. "What are

we to do now?" we asked God. "What ministry do You have for us?" The answer came with time. Adoption.

And so my life became focused on the telephone. I carried the phone everywhere I went in case the social worker called with answers about our questions or to tell us about a baby we could adopt. Later we waited for THE CALL informing us that it was time to fly to South Korea to bring our baby home.

Those months of knowing we had a baby on the other side of the world growing up without us were long and wearisome. When the phone hung silently day after long day, I cried. Then one day it did ring! And, oh, the joy! In a few days we were in Seoul holding our darling. All the paperwork, the training, the waiting, the long airplane flight, the sweat, the tears, were worth it. None of that mattered anymore. Our baby was in my arms!

Motherhood is hard work, much harder than I ever imagined. Some days I need to remind myself of how desperately I wanted this. Those of you who give birth, does this sound familiar? You have your labor, and I have mine. We are all mothers. Mothering is much the same in the end. Labor, weariness, sleepless nights, cooking, laundry, sewing, disciplining. Inexpressible love, hugs, kisses, joy at successes, laughter. God knows what it takes to make us what He wants us to be. For you it is biological children. For me it is adoption. I can't imagine having any other children than these. Thank you, Lord, for this reality.

The Mourning Dove Mother
by K. Regina Stauffer

I was weary. Weary of lugging 20 extra pounds of body weight with every step I took. Weary of getting up in the dead of night to use the bathroom, then being unable to get comfortable to go back to sleep. Weary of chasing my 18-month-old son around the house; he took advantage of Mom's lack of speed and enjoyed it. I was weary of this pregnancy.

One morning I slid out of bed and stretched awkwardly as I peered through the bedroom curtain at the foggy outdoors. The morning mist foretold a chilly, rainy day. The huge branches of the maple tree nearby swayed in the wind, and a few of its leaves brushed my window as if they, too, wanted to come inside to be warmed. When my eyes focused, I noticed a few drops of rain already splattering the sill, and I shivered. This morning I needed to buy groceries and stop at the pharmacy, but in this weather? *I might as well. I already waddle like a duck; the puddles and splashing raindrops will complete the picture—a mother duck followed by a small duckling in tiny yellow boots.*

I shivered again and yawned. I was about to turn away from the window when I detected a slight movement in the tree. There, nestled in the crook of two branches, was a tiny gray bird. A mourning dove! Sitting on a nest! I gasped as the comparison hit me: this bird was also "trapped" in the responsibility of incubating a tiny bit of life. There she sat, in the chilling rain, but she *didn't even consider* deserting her post! She wasn't questioning the wisdom of her Maker Who planned this forfeiture of freedom as part of motherhood.

Morning after morning, before I started my daily responsibilities, I checked up on my little friend the mourning dove. Without fail, I would find her in the crook of that tree, feathers unruffled, peace on her face—and in her heart—if that is possible in the bird kingdom. She did not waste one moment in doubting this was her place to fill. She embraced motherhood, yes, even if it meant being "tied down" to the nest in the tree. When the rest of the world was stirring to new life and new opportunities, she sat confined, for the sake of her young. She was absent from soaring over fresh green fields, finding nourishing seeds near the rich earthy soil, and drinking deeply from mountain springs while tiny crocuses blinked sleepy eyes and awakened nearby. But she left that all to her mate, willingly. She didn't think that life was unfair, or that motherhood was a cumbersome responsibility. She didn't resent her mate for his apparent freedom. She was simply and humbly fulfilling her Creator's will.

I cannot say that I never again complained about the increasing discomfort of pregnancy and the sacrifices I was making. It didn't happen quickly or completely, but with God's help in those laborious days, I tried to see motherhood as a noble calling. God was using the mourning dove to change my perspective. The mother bird nested there each day until my pregnancy ended in the birth of a precious baby girl. I have no doubt that God sent the little bird to teach me a lesson. I never saw the additions to her family; I was too busy with mine. But one morning, I paused at the window and noticed the vacant spot in the tree. I whispered, "Thank you, little bird, for your example in untiring commitment. Blessings to your little family! Goodbye! And, thank you, God!"

The Things Mothers Do
by Sarah Martin

As I bent down to untie a long strip of material from the release lever on my ironing board today, a strip my son tied on over 18 months ago, it struck me, the things mothers do, or don't do. That perfectly non-functional strip was there so long simply because I never took the time to untie it—I didn't get around to it. I started thinking about the things we don't get around to doing. And the things we do "get around to" doing . . .

. . . We hardly find time to read our Bibles some days, but rarely a day goes by that we don't read Golden books and bedtime stories.

. . . We don't get around to wiping the smudged windows but you might see us patiently cleaning smudges from cheap sunglasses, more than once a day.

. . . We don't get the floors washed every week, but we sit on those floors and put puzzles together with our preschoolers.

. . . We don't get around to washing the dishes 'til mid-morning, but we rarely forget to wash sticky fingers and faces after a meal.

. . . We don't get to visit neighbors and friends as much as we wish we could, but we crawl into precarious little tents and neatly-set-up rec room houses to visit our young daughters.

. . . We rush around before church or town trips, getting everyone presentable, then get out to the van and realize we forgot our own coat.

. . . We don't get around to weeding the flower bed, but we're found picking dandelions with our little ones out on the lawn.

We visit with our school-age children, maybe this one, maybe that one, while we rock the baby much longer than necessary and the house is a mess. We play Memory and Uno every day, while the scrapbook page waits. We hang up crayoned pictures and indistinguishable works of art, and only admire the lovely framed paintings in the store from a distance. We decorate with wilted bunches of violets and sparkly rocks, brought lovingly in grimy fists. Our days are unpredictable at best. Our grand resolutions and lofty goals get buried beneath the ceaseless clutter of crayons, marbles, odd socks, cracker crumbs, sippy cups, dirty dishes, papers, tools, and toys.

Why do Moms do such strange things? Why do we pay attention to such little things, yet some obvious duties are, at least temporarily, neglected? Why do we try so hard to be okay with schedules gone awry and work that sits undone?

It's because we are raising children. We have learned that what might seem important to some, is really not the most important of all. It's because our children won't remember so much whether or not the windows were shining or the floors spotless; they will remember if Mom had time for them, if she was patient and cheerful, if their projects and games and little treasures were important to her.

In spite of knowing all that, I have to admit, sometimes my life feels so mundane, so repetitious and normal. I wonder, *What am I really doing that counts?* Everything I do is so soon undone. I do it all again and again, and who notices? Food that took hours to prepare is gone in minutes. Clothes get laundered, folded, and put in drawers today only to land in the hamper again tomorrow. Cleaning gets done so everyone can come along and start over with fresh dirt. Special projects, when they happen, happen with two or more not-very-helpful helpers breathing over my shoulder. Exercise time turns into a slow stroll while we stop after every other step to scrutinize some wonder of nature. I have even been guilty of saying to my husband, "I didn't do anything of lasting value today!"

    I need to remind myself time and again that all these daily duties, repetitious and insignificant, are but side notes in the great responsibility of raising souls. And if one soul is worth more than the whole world, what glory should attend the mundane tasks I do! The all-encompassing goal of these "normal" days is to teach of God, to establish relationships that will continue to bless us long after this labor-intensive stage is past. When I look at the big picture and what really matters to God, then suddenly the "unimportant" things I do seem very important indeed! The tasks I repeat day after day are of lasting value. They are creating an environment in which the seeds of love, respect, trust, time, and companionship can grow. The joy with which I attend to my children and my husband will be apparent, and make those seeds to germinate more quickly, and become robust and healthy. As I think upon these things, a prayer springs up in my heart; "Lord, I want to sweep grimy floors, empty overflowing clothes hampers again and yet again, prepare with joy these foods that so quickly will disappear, wipe sticky fingers and runny noses over and over, play childish games, pick weeds for my bouquets, admire dolls and wooden creations, decorate my walls and refrigerator with crayon art and multiple papers, and smile through it all. I want to enjoy my family, to fulfil to the best of my ability this great calling of motherhood, to savor the moments and sing to the babies. Thank You, thank You for common, ordinary days whose 'little' tasks are so great!"

Out of the Mouth of Babes
by L. D. Nolt

*"And Jesus saith unto them, Yea;
have ye never read, Out of the mouth of babes
and sucklings thou hast perfected praise?"
-Matthew 21:16b*

In a conversation with my husband at the supper table, I mentioned feeling a bit "down in the dumps." It wasn't something I said with a lot of thought, although it was true and I was having a hard time keeping a positive focus. Our four young children gathered with us at the table, usually have open ears, which is what caused my six-year-old daughter to comment on my words.

The conversation had already moved on, when she said, "Mom, you aren't the only one down in the dumps."

It took me a little to realize what she was saying. "What do you mean? Are you down in the dumps?" I asked, wondering what she was thinking.

"No," she said, "but God is with you in the dumps. He's everywhere."

My eight-year-old son added, "We are never alone, right Mom?"

"That's right," my husband and I agreed, giving each other a meaningful look. And then so quickly the topic was changed and their little voices blended together, discussing school and other little people topics.

My mind, of course, couldn't move past the words of wisdom from my children. *You are not alone. God is everywhere.* The words of Jesus in Matthew 21:16 ran through my mind, "out of the mouth of babes and sucklings thou hast perfected praise."

How dare I wallow in the "dumps," I thought with shame. *My faith is more sure than that. I have been failing to see that God is able. I am allowing myself to be drug down by the evil one.* My thoughts raced on.

The wisdom of children is totally remarkable to me. In their innocence their faith is perfect. They don't doubt that God is there. They don't worry about the future needlessly, they know they are well cared for. Their trust is without question. Once taught of God and His goodness, they can grasp it better than adults can. Their belief is pure and deep. That is why it is so dangerous for parents to ever teach anything that is not true. Children believe what they are told with all their hearts.

Created in God's own imagine we are His children. His creation. And His desire is to see us bring forth "perfected praise." As innocent children, their praise to God is perfect. Why else would Jesus have said, "Except ye be converted, and become as little children, ye shall not enter into the kingdom of heaven."

I have often been encouraged by my children. I truly believe that God often guides and speaks to us through our children. Are we willing to listen? Our children are our heritage from the Lord. Given to us from God with the purpose of raising them for His glory.

I encourage you to teach and then listen to the faith of your children. They can inspire you to return to a positive faith. To bring forth "perfect praise." I always liked this quote by A. W. Tozer, "While we are looking at God, we do not see ourselves, which is blessed riddance."

When you are feeling down in the dumps, you can rest assured that God is with you. He will never leave you, nor forsake you. His desire is for you to trust Him whether in good times or bad.

Out of the mouth of a six year old, "You aren't the only one down in the dumps." God is always near! Our children can sometimes be God's mouthpiece. Let them speak to you!

Dear Son
by Brenda Petre

My head is heavy, and my arms
    are aching, holding you—
Dear little son, so wide awake
    with eyes so softly blue.

If only I could drift to sleep
    in undisturbed repose!
How long must I keep rocking you
    until your eyelids close?

Dear little one, we love you so.
    We thank the Lord for you;
We hope you'll grow to be a man
    who's faithful, kind and true.

There are so many things to choose,
    so much that you must learn,
And Satan's goal is that your feet
    someday from God would turn.

Dear son, to hold you to my heart
    is easier by far,
Than if I'd have to lie awake
    and wonder where you are.

This Is Life
by K. Regina Stauffer

I snatch up the newspaper from the kitchen table, lest the headlines grab the attention of my second grader doing his homework. "It's okay, Mom," he says with the air of a 14 year old. He is trying to reassure me. "I heard the big boys at school talking about that. They said a man with a mask and a gun came into a school and shot a lot of little children and some teachers." His eyes search my face.

It shouldn't have to be this way, but it is. We live in a sin-cursed world.

"Why didn't Christie's daddy come to Grandma's house for our Christmas supper?" our son wonders.

"He wasn't along when we sang for the neighbors last month, either," our daughter comments. It's an honest question. It deserves an honest answer. But how do you explain to trusting seven and eight year olds that Christie's daddy is spending Christmas with another mom and her children? And that's why Grandma and Grandpa, Christie's mom—the whole family—didn't have a happy Christmas?

It shouldn't have to be this way, but it is. We live in a fallen world.

I show a six-year-old wedding photo to my children. Pointing to the groom, I tell them, "Here is the daddy who was killed. It's the daddy that the little girl and little boy lost." Just weeks later, we huddle near the grave of yet another dad who was snatched from this life. As the dirt clods plunk onto the coffin lid, the man's teenage son bows his head and weeps for what was, and for what will never be.

It shouldn't have to be this way. We live in a sin-cursed world.

The four children and I are hurrying around the grocery store, ticking items off the list against the time pressure of lunchtime and naps. My bored toddler lifts up the cereal box that he had been sitting on and tosses it into the aisle. Another shopper kindly picks up the box for us. I am shocked, not by her thoughtful deed, but by her inadequate way of dress that becomes even more glaring when she bends down for the box right next to my wide-eyed children. We have another drill on "Drop Your Eyes" as we drive home from the store.

It shouldn't have to be this way, but it is. We live in a fallen world.

Headlines in the local paper relate the murder of our young neighbor, the mother of eight-year-old Vicki. The killer was none other than Vicki's father. Suddenly the small girl is thrust into an unfamiliar home, her mother dead and her father behind bars for the remainder of his life.

It shouldn't have to be this way, but it is. We live in a fallen world.

My daughters resume their dollhouse play while I clean up the lunch dishes. My whistling stops abruptly, however, when I overhear a little sister being told, "No, you can't have two mommies in one house! Every house should have one dad, one mom, and maybe children." My daughter trots into the kitchen to dry dishes. She giggles. "Aleah is funny. She had two moms living in the same house." I smile, too; my first grader is correct—living like that is not right. But I am sobered by the fact that in a few years our children will discover that our government condones exactly that kind of lifestyle.

It shouldn't have to be this way, but we live in a fallen world.

I am sitting in the lobby of a doctor's office, waiting for an appointment. It's unusual that I would drag four children with me to one child's appointment, but then, this *whole day* has been unusual. When my son fell and gashed his chin on our stepladder, I didn't have time to find a babysitter in the 15 minutes before we fled the house. Now, I sigh in relief that we've come this far. I can relax a bit, with each child settled on a designated chair.

They are being a bit *too* angelic, so I investigate and realize with horror that four little pairs of eyes are affixed to a TV screen with awful images flashing across it. An atrocious being plunges a glittering weapon into the chest of his enemy. There is blood . . . "Children!" I exclaim, and they jump, startled, and we re-situate on the row of chairs behind us. When I sink into a chair for the second time, my eyes connect with a second monster. It reminds me of the Bible verse that describes Satan as a roaring, prowling lion. For, there, poking out of the wall and uninvited by me, is a second TV. This one flaunts several youth at the beach, which spells immodesty and a lifestyle from which we want to shield our children.

What should I do now? Before long, a silly cartoon replaces it but I'm still relieved when the nurse calls my son for his appointment. We tramp along behind her; some of the family is walking backwards because they aren't finished watching.

We live in a sin-cursed world.

Broken relationships, morals spiraling downwards, blatant undress, legalized sin, violence. . . . <u>The lion is out</u>! And he is seeking to destroy the faith of the remnant. Our minister reminds us, "We send our children into a future that we ourselves will not see," and I shudder involuntarily. This job looks too big! I want to turn and run from the responsibility. I cringe and pray, **Lord Jesus, come quickly!**

But we can't give up now! Until His return—or *because of* His sure return—parents, we need to be on our guard constantly! Take courage. Take the Word of God in one hand and your child's hand in the other. Explain to them why we do the things we do, why we don't do *that*, and why we feel it's wrong. **Remind your children that God loves them no matter what may happen.** Show them Jesus' words, make the Bible personal to them, and hide The Word in their hearts. Teach them to pray as soon as they are able to talk. The things of the world that shock our generation today could easily become the normal for our children to view tomorrow. We must prepare them!

> *What doth the LORD require of thee,*
> *but to do justly, and to love mercy,*
> *and to walk humbly with thy God?*
> *-Micah 6:8*

> *And thou shalt teach them diligently unto thy children, and shalt talk of them when thou sittest in thine house, and when thou walkest by the way, and when thou liest down, and when thou risest up. -Deut. 6:7*

What Color Is Grass, Anyway?
(And Does It Really Matter?)
by Sue Hooley

What we consider normal is often determined by our frame of reference. For example, after we moved to eastern Oregon from the green rolling terrain of central Virginia, a friend wondered how we liked the new scenery. "We really like it," I offered. "But we do miss the lush green countryside."

"This *is* green!" She laughed, "I moved here from dull brown-green Arizona and in comparison this is so much greener. Isn't interesting how our childhood locations have an effect on how we view the color of grass?"

Our experiences can affect how we view our circumstances or the situation of others. A few years ago I had a miscarriage just before the Christmas holidays. In an effort to raise my spirits I decided to go Christmas caroling with my family. It was difficult to sing and harder yet to identify with Mary. Song after song was about Mary and her baby. *Stable or not, at least she had her baby*, I concluded.

A few years passed and once again it was time for Christmas caroling. I had recently given birth to a darling baby girl and happy thoughts flitted through my mind as I listened. *Mary and her baby, I and my baby* . . . Then the words of a familiar song floated through the wintery air, "Away in a manger, no crib for His bed . . ." What? No crib for her baby? "The cattle are lowing . . ."

She gave birth to her first baby in a dirty smelly barn with cows and horses? As I considered the reality of Mary's situation, I thought of my own experience. *My baby arrived in a cozy atmosphere surrounded by knowledgeable assistants. I had clean sheets, fresh water and a temperature-controlled room. How did Mary do it?*

My experiences affected how I viewed the stable. In my grief, I could easily overlook its conditions. In my state of happiness, I could more clearly understand its imperfections.

Perhaps it is easy to understand two emotional views. However, it can become more complex when two or more people have a contrasting frame of reference on a particular subject. Then it affects *"how I do it"* or *"how they do it"* or even more complicated, *"how we do it."* For example, when children blow out the candles on their birthday cakes, some adults see fun and memories and others see germs and saliva. Why the difference? Likely, childhood traditions shape the way we observe the "wind and the rain." Some may have blown out the candles multiple times at each sibling's birthday. In other situations, perhaps only the birthday child blew out the candles to minimize the chance of spreading germs.

Community values are different. In one area purchasing quality fruit for canning is a priority. *"If you are going to pick it, pare it, add sugar, and process it, your time will only be worth it if you buy fruit of highest quality."* In another community, money is the issue and it does not seem to matter if the flavor is missing nor if a third of it needs to be tossed to the pigs.

Friends do not always think alike. Past experiences can cause them to look at the same thing very differently. I have a friend who would love to have a pond or a rushing creek. I look at that as a potential hazard and if we had a pond, it would be securely fenced. In my younger years, several of my girlfriends lost siblings in drowning accidents, but my friend doesn't have any personal connections to a drowning.

Our personalities, childhood home, things we were taught

or not taught, the school we attended, social peers, geographical location, our in-laws, and church settings can influence our way of doing things or even what we deem as important. We are not identical and we all have different backgrounds, therefore we will not do things alike. Really, does it matter if premium or inferior fruit is preserved? Or if no fruit is preserved at all?

Sometimes we get so burdened with the methods of other women that we forget that they are serving the Lord. As women our tendency is to compare ourselves with others and become judgmental or easily intimidated. It may not be pride that motivates Anne to traditionally sew a new dress for her girls on the first day of school. Maybe her deceased mother did that for her and it is a special memory. Is it possible that Hilda uses a dryer because her husband dislikes stiff clothes and towels and not because she is lazy? Perhaps Mable walks into your house without knocking because that was acceptable in the community she moved from; she may not be rude at all.

Sisters in the Lord should have a sense of loyalty to each other. Regardless of methods, every woman that is serving the Lord has qualities that we can learn from. We owe it to our sisters to speak kindly and accurately about them. Attitudes of jealousy, inferiority or superiority can cause us to put a false motive into the life of our sister. Proverbs 4:23 says, *Keep thy heart with all diligence; for out of it are the issues of life.*

Just like the varying shades of green grass, God created woman with varied personalities and gifts. If we can learn to enjoy a new terrain, certainly we can learn to respect the methods and preferences of other women. Romans 12:10 says, *Be kindly affectioned one to another with [sisterly] love; in honour preferring one another.* And that is what really matters.

What I Learned From the Birth of Our First Baby
(What I Plan to Do Differently with the Next)
by Crystal Steinhauer

I had heard having a child is life-changing. *Life-changing*. What a bland way to describe all normals being stuffed into a blender and whipped at high speed. Sure, I was excited about having a baby, but I was not prepared for how drastically my life would change overnight—literally.

That was a year and a half ago—a wonderful year and a half ago. And now I'm at the brink of going through this birth experience all over again, a little wiser now, perhaps, although there is no way to know what hairpin curves may lie ahead.

Stock up. Surely, I thought, nothing could be as liberating as not being pregnant anymore. I would have boundless energy to do everything such as shopping, something my heavily laden body complained about. Not true. Five days after our daughter's birth, I was at Wal-mart because I was almost out of disposable diapers (shouldn't a box of 72 last a long time?). And groceries. And shampoo. I never realized how huge Wal-mart is until that day. My post-partum body was worn out when I was done.

This time, I've been spreading out the stocking-up process over several months (so as not to tax our budget), coming home with a case of toilet paper one week, a box of diapers the next. It's my goal to have a stockpile of health and beauty supplies and non-perishable groceries so that if I have to send my husband, mom, or maid to the store, it will be only for things like milk or fresh produce.

*Prepare a **variety** of meals for the freezer.* Before our first child, I wanted some food in the freezer, so one day I made a large batch of chicken-etti and divided it into meal-sized portions—six of them. My husband liked chicken-etti. Notice the past tense—*liked*. Not only did we have our six portions of chicken-etti to get through, our neighbor kindly brought us a large portion of it as well. I haven't made it since.

Several weeks ago, I purchased a stack of foil pans and instead of making a large batch of one food, I've been putting two or three meals in the freezer a week, doubles of what we have that night for supper. In addition, I made a batch of breakfast burritos and granola bars for the freezer—quick grabs for after the 5 a.m. feeding when I'm faint with hunger.

Relax, relax, relax. I was ashamed when a friend stopped in one day near lunchtime and there I was, still in my housecoat, hair uncombed. I felt guilty when my mom came and took over my housework. I was embarrassed when she and dad pulled and processed all the corn that was ready in my garden the week after my baby was born. I hadn't planned on needing any help. I felt I should help with the dishes, prepare the treat for our visitors, and carry the laundry to the basement.

Now that I have another child underfoot and more realistic expectations, I arranged for a maid to come several times a week for three weeks after the baby's birth, and then once a week for another two. I will (try to) enjoy my vacation while I feed my baby and read to my toddler, and let my maid do the housework.

Have distractions ready for the baby blues. I'm not the weepy type. I could count on one hand the times I cried for no reason since we were married. So I was surprised—*shocked*—when I had no control over my emotions the first two weeks after our bundle arrived. Toward afternoon, a helpless feeling overwhelmed me.

Any stimuli opened the floodgates. My dear husband just held me and let me cry, realizing there was nothing he could do to fix it. Someone suggested having a distraction—a good book, perhaps—for those weepy moments. I found that helped a lot.

I have three books saved and waiting for this baby's arrival—a devotional book for mothers and two storybooks that were highly recommended to me. (No sad books though!)

Remember each stage is just that—a stage. For the first time in our one year of marriage, I went to bed alone the night we brought our baby home from the hospital. I was exhausted, and she was not interested in sleeping anywhere but our arms, so my husband told me to go to bed. He would tend to the baby. I felt so alone in that big queen-sized bed that I returned to the living room sobbing. My husband solved the problem by coming and staying with me until I was asleep. But it wasn't only that one night our baby wasn't interested in sleeping. For a week or two she settled around 1:00 a.m., and we were often in bed only a few hours at the same time, my husband taking the first shift and I getting up the rest of the night.

Those nights are a distant memory now. Our daughter started sleeping through the night at nine weeks and while I have to occasionally go to her room and soothe her after a bad dream, I'm back to bed in several minutes. When I'm up with our next child for the fifth time in one night and feel like I will never be able to stay in bed all night again, I will remind myself: This too shall pass.

Prioritize time with Christ. In my new and unpredictable role as mother, a neat half-hour morning slot of uninterrupted time for my devotions just didn't happen. Often I would get to the end of the day and realize I'd forgotten the most important part!

Realistically, a new baby means I may only be able to meditate on the verse on the wall motto, my day-to-day calendar, or planner. It may just be a quick plea to not get frustrated with my toddler, a breath of thanks for freshly-bathed baby skin, but I must allow my mind to rise above the earthly and get a glimpse of the Bigger Picture.

Will the things I've learned guarantee a smooth and successful transition to being a mother of two? No, but maybe they'll help. And by the time we are waiting for a third little person, there will be another article waiting to be written: *Things I Learned from the Birth of Our Second Baby—What I Plan to Do Differently With the Third.*

Childish Trust
by Brenda Petre

I rub his pudgy little arm
Until he goes to sleep,
Because I understand his fear
Of darkness cold and deep;
And little dreams that seem so real
And terrify his mind.
I want his heart to trust in me
And think that I am kind.
Oh Father, often have I come
With terrifying fears,
And in the darkness felt Your hand
Just brush away my tears;
Help me to be as good to him
As you have been to me,
And may he feel the love I feel
When it's too dark to see.

WHAT IF GOD SAYS NO?
by L. D. Nolt

I watched the snowflakes spin through the air dizzily. Wiping tears from my eyes I shivered. The weather was perfect for this day.

Standing outside the church I waited my turn to pass through the line to view the body of our infant neighbor. His little life only lasted just over three weeks, all of it spent in Hershey Medical Center. As amazing as the medical field is, they couldn't change the will of God. This time God said, "No."

My mother-heart hurts for the parents. Even though this little one was a twin and his brother is healthy, their arms will still ache and the dreams they had for this baby will need to be laid to rest along with his little body. They will need to let go—to hold onto faith even when it hurts so bad and the disappointment is so keen.

As I watched the many supporters of this family file past I pondered prayers that we as mothers offer up on behalf of our children or husbands. We pray daily for their safety, their health, and place them in the protection of the Father. But sometimes God says, "No."

My mind went to another dear friend of mine who just underwent brain surgery for a tumor and is facing an unknown future. She is so young; a mother also, I am sure she prayed for health, for God's protection. But for reasons known only to the Almighty, He chose to have her walk a different route; and said "no" to health for now.

All of us that serve our Heavenly Father have been told "no" at some point in our lives. Maybe He has said "no" to a new job or a purchase of a farm, or even to a long anticipated move. Maybe His "no" had to do with having children or the healing of a dear loved one. Maybe you heard Him say "no" when you desperately prayed for a "yes." And maybe, like this baby, God said "no" and withdrew His protection on one of your children or friends and took them home to be with Him.

In raising a family, we have to say "no" to our children many times. Their carnal nature often pops up and they question why. They can't understand why they can't do this or that when others may be allowed. Sometimes we can't explain all the whys to them, they just need to take us at our word and trust that our "no" is for their own good. Sometimes it hurts our hearts to tell them no, but we know we have to.

So what if God says "No." Does it mean He loves us less? No, it just means He knows what is the best for us. Isn't it enough we have His grace and that we know that His love will never fail? Even through deep grief His grace is sufficient and we can take Him at His Word, "I will never leave thee, nor forsake thee." (Hebrew 13:5)

Jesus prayed on that last night before He was crucified; "Lord, let this cup pass from me" But God saw the big picture and knew that it had to be done; so as much as it hurt His Father-heart, He couldn't even say "yes" to His own Son. Aren't we so grateful He said no? Because of that we can now have eternal life through Jesus' blood He shed for our sins!

We can't always see the benefit of a "no" from God, but we cannot let go of our faith when that "no" comes. Trust Him. His grace is sufficient—even when He says "no."

"And he said unto me, My grace is sufficient for thee: for my strength is made perfect in weakness."
-2 Cor. 12:9a

SOLITUDE
by Faith Sommers

I was born with an aptitude for solitude. To explain: I liked to be alone. Oh, I like to be with people, too, and love meeting new friends. But to have a few hours to myself? Wonderful!

Once, when I was very small, I was engrossed in a wondrous play with my doll family. So much so that my real people family gathered up and left to sing for someone . . . and I never found out. Until they returned for me, perhaps 15 minutes later, my mother praying that I wouldn't be frantic and sobbing.

Not to worry. I "awakened" to hear the crunch of gravel, so I pulled back the curtains of the upstairs window to see who was coming. I was so puzzled. It was our van, and out piled my mother, and father, sisters and brother looking for me! I was safe and happy all the while.

When I was in my teens, I found the verse in Psalm 68: "He setteth the solitary in families." I decided God definitely meant that verse for me. In solitude, I could be close to God, but it didn't teach me how to respond graciously to others, how to be socially acceptable, and how to cook a decent meal.

Pass the years—a little less than 40 of them. For 20 of the years, I have been surrounded by noise, activity and little bodies who need attention, love and care.

God provides strength for the journey of raising children for Him, and joy in many situations and times. I survived! And so did they!

Insert here that my husband soon learned that on some days his love for me meant that he juggled home duties and bathed babies while I went to the grocery store. In a few moments here and there quietude was found, and my sanity sustained.

Now our youngest child is in first grade. Our oldest daughter taught school for a few months last year, while the youngest was in kindergarten, so the house was very quiet.

One of the first times I had an all-day shopping trip *by myself*, I commented that it felt "weird." My littlest daughter heard. She felt so sorry for me. She's a true "youngest child." Her heart is happiest when she is surrounded by people.

So she was torn when the opportunity arose to go with her daddy one evening. The four oldest children left to help a neighbor and my husband planned to pick up his nephew at the airport. Our youngest son immediately wanted to go with him, and I said of course.

Daughter was in a quandary. She went searching for shoes, and then came back to the kitchen. "Mama, I don't know what I should do. Shall I go with Daddy, or stay with you?"

I assured her that she could go, and she bounced out to the car. Within moments she was back, this time in tears. Why the tears?

"I can't decide what to do. I kinda want to go, but then you'll be all by yourself."

"I will be fine," I said, hiding a smile.

"I kinda want to stay with you." (Pitiful wail.)

"Then you may!"

A honk from the car horn. She ran out.

And returned.

This time Daddy came, too. "Listen, you can't go with me AND stay with Mama. You may do whatever you want, but you Must Stop Crying. And hurry. We have to leave. Now."

She took a third run to the car. And returned the third time.

Trying hard to wipe the tears that Daddy forbade, she said again, "But you'll be All Alone."

(And what's so bad about that? Did she really never detect how much I enjoyed being alone? I suppose because she hates an empty house, she assumes everyone does.)

"What will you DO when we're gone?"

"Actually," I said, stifling a sigh, "I will do the supper dishes. Then I want to clean the upstairs."

Her tears dried magically. The decision was suddenly easy. Off she went.

I chuckled later as I told my sister about it. My daughter overheard this conversation, too. A bit shamefacedly, she said, "But Mama, once you said it was weird to go to town alone."

"Yes, but it was a good weird!" I gave her a big hug. She giggled. And she doesn't worry about me anymore. Not too much.

Measured in Moments
by Faith Sommers

Where are the hours of heartfelt sharing? The days of games and family fun?

"Spend time with your children," is admonition often heard.

Guilt threatens to overwhelm my spirit with its dark shadow. I don't spend hours daily with each child. Do I even have a few minutes alone with each?

The child in me begs to run and jump, clamor and climb all day, every day, with this darling energetic group of youngsters God placed within our care.

The housekeeper (I call her Martha) within must also be heard. What about the cooking, the baking, the cleaning, the mending?

What about the gifts of painting, writing, crocheting? From God, I am assured.

Puzzled, I struggle to find a balance. To know what I should do, what I must do, what I can do.

And in the midst of cleaning, hope arises.

A little one dusts, I scrub; another vacuums, I mop. When we bake, they roll out cookies, and frost cakes. We do laundry as a team.

When I paint, they practice with fingerpaints. My stamping card hobby becomes theirs. My stitches inspire our daughters to sew a button or two.

We ARE spending time together! And we do have time to play. We race together for a target, we make a game out of cleaning, we play

"Memory" while the bread rises, "I Spy" when it's dark and rainy; we swing and take turns to push; we learn to bat a ball, and even to catch it.

Stories read aloud become family favorites. Poems and songs learned while traveling become special, too. Verses memorized become a challenge.

Cuddle moments when a child awakens, kisses at bedtime . . . all these are tiny moments tucked here and there in the big, busy day. But these moments count. We love each other. Each moment we share becomes another pearl in my heart-basket of Treasured Memories.

OF CHILDREN AND FLOORS
by Darla Weaver

The floor was clean an hour ago,
I loved to see it shine.
Freshly swept and freshly washed,
The sparkle looked so fine.
The floor was clean an hour ago,
When I was home alone.
The rugs were straight, the toys away,
And every corner shone.

The floor was clean an hour ago,
Alas, it is no more.
It's cluttered, tracked, and not-so-clean,
Just like it was before.
The children have come home again,
And though I love clean floors,
I grin and bear the dirt and all—
I love my children more.

Dandelion Bouquets
by Regina Rosenberry

My little boy of three stands before me, clad in denim overalls and yellow-ducky boots. His eyes sparkle from behind crooked glasses as he asks, "Guess what I have?" I notice then, his hands are hidden behind his back.

"A bug?" I answer. He grins and shakes his head.

"A worm?" His grin gets bigger, but again, a no.

"Is it a flower?" This time, I am rewarded with a chubby hand stretched towards me. A small bouquet of dandelions is clenched in his fist.

"I love flowers!" I take the slightly-smashed offering from his hand and smile into his eyes.

His dirt-smudged cheeks smile back. "I like picking flowers for you, Mom," he says and runs back to his red training-wheel bike.

I watch him go and think: *Can anything be sweeter to a mom than the first love-picked dandelion bouquet of spring?* Their bright, sunshiny yellows peek out from among the new green of the grass, inviting little fingers to pick them. I wondered then if God created dandelions just for this reason?

I brush the bent petals across my cheek enjoying their fuzziness, and my heart is warmed by the love in these simple flowers. *Hmm, could this perhaps be how God feels when I do something special for Him?* When my day is already bursting with duties, but I take a moment to visit with the lonely neighbor lady, or give the grocery lady a smile and a hello? Maybe when I stop my sewing to read a story to that little boy in the yellow-ducky boots or to give him a special "I love you" hug; does God feel as if I just picked Him a dandelion bouquet? Does He see the beauty in an act of kindness no matter how small and is His heart warmed and pleased?

As I smell the dandelions' sweet and musty scent, I realize that an offering of love, no matter how simple, brings us some of life's greatest joy. I determine within me to pick more dandelions for my Father.

Spend and Be Spent
by Janice Etter

I will not stop praying for you, my son;
I will spend and be spent for you.
I love with a love that will not relent—
Love that is meant for you.

Though I long for peace, I can never yield;
I will keep my arrows flying.
Until they have pierced your armored shield,
I cannot cease from trying.

I see you kick at your conscience-pricks;
You believe you will never bend,
But until you do, I will spend for you
What I have in my heart to spend.

Send Them to School With a Smile

by Faith Sommers

Oh, mother, so weary of rising
    Before the sun beams its bright ray,
To ready the children, and send them
    Off for another school day . . .

The breakfast, so simple yet hearty
    Is needful to strengthen their hearts,
But more so the family devotions,
    To nourish, and each shares a part.

The morning chores must be completed,
    The animals cared for and fed;
House tidied, floors swept and rugs shaken;
    Wash dishes, and make all the beds.

Help Sister find food for the lunch box . . .
    Oh, have you grown tired of stew?
Be thankful for milk and canned peaches . . .
    Determine to bake after school.

Now scramble to find coats or jackets,
    Boots, mittens and scarves when it's cold;
Find schoolbooks, check nails, ears and faces—
    Each clean, shining visage behold.

In all of the hurried morn schedule
    Remember the things that will count,
A cheerful and calm loving mother
    Will all hectic moments surmount.

A smile for the child who is leaving
    Will brighten his day all the while,
He'll sooner be kind to his classmates
    Because mom remembered to smile!

Their burdens will seem so much lighter,
    When they have a home filled with love,
And homes with the Lord as the Master
    Are homes blessed by heaven above.